CLASSIC *f*M

THE CLASSIC FM QUIZ BOOK

DARREN HENLEY AND TIM LIHOREAU

First published 2012 by Elliott and Thompson Limited
27 John Street, London WC1N 2BX
www.eandtbooks.com

ISBN: 978-1-908739-18-6

9 8 7 6 5 4 3 2 1

A catalogue record for this book is available from the British Library

Printed and bound in the UK by TJ International Ltd

Cover design by Kai and Sunny
Typeset by PDQ Digital Media Solutions Ltd, Bungay

CONTENTS

INTRODUCTION

It seems hard to believe that it was twenty years ago that we first turned on Classic FM's transmitters. Those two decades of playing classical music to the nation have absolutely raced by, but then they do say that time flies when you're having fun. In the intervening years, we have had the privilege of sharing the world's greatest music with millions of people right across the UK.

If you listen hard enough, classical music is everywhere, all around us. We're just as likely to hear it on television, at the cinema, at football grounds and in restaurants as we are on CDs, on our iPods, in the concert hall or by listening to a classical music radio station such as Classic FM.

We hope that we have played a small part in continuing to democratize classical music over the past two decades. We have always believed that it can and should be a part of everyone's lives – no matter who they are or where they come from. That's why you will always find programmes on Classic FM that explain the history and development of classical music. It's also why much of our website, classicfm.com, is dedicated to taking online listeners on a journey of discovery through the genre.

Over the past few years, along with Classic FM's Managing Editor Sam Jackson, we have written several books: *Classic Ephemera*, *The Classic FM Hall of Fame*, and *Everything You Ever Wanted To Know About Classical Music … But Were Too Afraid To Ask*. We hope that these have helped to provide listeners to our radio station and users of our website with an even deeper understanding of the subject.

To mark our 20th birthday, we thought it would be fun to publish this book as a companion volume to the others. We've set out to create the classical music quiz book that has something for everyone. So, no matter if you are just dipping a toe gingerly into the classical music waters, or if you have been basking in all of classical music's glories for years; you will find questions that you can answer in the next 130 or so pages.

This book is made up of 1,150 questions, divided into a series of rounds. As you will see, some of the rounds require straight general knowledge about classical music; other rounds use a number of tried and tested quiz formats, such as working on the basis of mixing and matching answers given on the page, or by asking whether statements are true or false. We have graded all of the Quick Fire rounds as being *Easier*, *Intermediate* or *Fiendish*, depending on the level of difficulty we believe you will have in answering the question. You will find that the *Easier* rounds of this type are towards the front of the book, with the *Fiendish* ones being towards the back. Also, look out for our five rounds of *Enigmas*, which have become a regular feature on Classic FM's *More Music Breakfast* presented by Tim Lihoreau every weekday morning between 6am and 9am.

Once you've answered all of the questions, you can score yourself by checking out the answers section at the back of the book.

Good luck! And remember the old adage that any quiz question is easy … as long as you know the answer.

THE ROUNDS

THE QUESTIONS

Round 1: Quick Fire (Easier)

1. If "legato" is a request by a composer to a performer to play the music smoothly, what does "staccato" mean?

2. What does the word "opera" actually mean?

3. Spell the Polish composer Henryk Górecki's surname phonetically.

4. What is the name of the piece of instrumental music played at the beginning of an opera, which often includes musical themes heard later on?

5. What are the names of The Three Tenors?

6. Which flautist became known as "the man with the golden flute" in the 1970s and 1980s?

7. The name of the instrument, "piano", is short for the Italian word "pianoforte". What does that translate as?

8. In the popular children's story by Paul Tripp, what sort of instrument is Tubby?

9. Leonard Bernstein wrote the music to *West Side Story*. Who wrote the words?

10. In which Suffolk seaside town, where he founded a music festival, did Benjamin Britten make his home?

11. Who is the current Master of the Queen's Music?

12. In 2007, Edward Elgar's 150th birthday year, the Bank of England decided to take him off the back of the £20 note. With whom did they replace him?

13. Tchaikovsky's *1812 Overture* celebrates the victory of which nation over which other nation?

14. How many symphonies did Franz Joseph Haydn compose?

15. He's famous now as a classical composer, but of which 1970s rock band was Karl Jenkins a member?

16. What family relationship did Felix and Fanny Mendelssohn have?

17. Which was written first – Frédéric Chopin's *Piano Concerto No. 1* or his *Piano Concerto No. 2*?

18. Name the piece of music composed by Maurice Ravel, which was made famous when Torvill and Dean won a gold medal at the 1984 Olympic Games in Sarajevo.

19. The dish Tournedos Rossini was named after the composer Gioachino Rossini. It consists of croutons with steak layered on top, along with which two other toppings?

20. In which English city is the composer John Rutter based?

Round 2: Cinematic Sounds

Match the film soundtrack composers to their films.

You can choose from:
49th Parallel, Alien, Dances with Wolves, Dangerous Moonlight, The Gadfly, Gladiator, The Heiress, Henry V (1944), The Hours, Lieutenant Kijé, The Lord of the Rings, The Magnificent Seven, The Mission, The Piano, Pride and Prejudice (2005), Robin Hood, Prince of Thieves, Sense and Sensibility, The Snowman, Superman, Titanic.

1. Richard Addinsell

2. John Barry

3. Elmer Bernstein

4. Howard Blake

5. Aaron Copland

6. Carl Davis

7. Patrick Doyle

8. Philip Glass

9. Jerry Goldsmith

10. James Horner

11. Michael Kamen

12. Ennio Morricone

13. Michael Nyman

14. Sergei Prokofiev

15. Dmitri Shostakovich

16. Howard Shore

17. Ralph Vaughan Williams

18. William Walton

19. John Williams

20. Hans Zimmer

🎵 **Round 3:** Quick Fire (Easier)

1. Which of Schubert's symphonies is known as being "*Unfinished*"?

2. What musical jobs did Robert Schumann's wife, Clara, do?

3. Who was known as "the Father of the Waltz"?

4. Who was known as "the Waltz King"?

5. Classic FM's first Composer in Residence, Joby Talbot, was once a member of which pop group?

6. By what nickname was Antonio Vivaldi known?

7. John Tavener and John Taverner are both English composers, but one was born around 450 years earlier than the other. Which was it?

8. Gregorian Chant was named after whom?

9. What is the name of the 12th-century nun who, as well as being a composer, also wrote poetry and was a famed mystic, having no fewer than 26 visions?

10. We talk about Renaissance music, but what is the literal translation of "Renaissance" from French into English?

11. The Belgian early music composer Guillaume Dufay wrote a mass based on a folk song called *The Armed Man*. What is the name of the 21st-century Welsh composer who had great success with his new work of the same name?

12. The early English composer John Taverner was friendly with the man who was one of the main forces behind the dissolution of the monasteries. What was the name of his friend?

13. What does "opus" literally mean?

14. Which body decreed that anybody who made an illegal copy of Gregorio Allegri's *Miserere* would be punished?

15. How did the composer Jean-Baptiste Lully die?

16. A piece written by the French composer Marc-Antoine Charpentier is always played at the beginning of the Eurovision Song Contest. What is its name?

17. The composer Arcangelo Corelli was the master of a particular type of concerto, where the orchestra is divided into two groups. One group of musicians tends to play first, with a second group then echoing the music played by the first set. What is this sort of concerto called?

18. *"Frère Jacques"*, *"Three Blind Mice"* and *"London's Burning"* all have something in common with Johann Pachelbel's most famous work. What is it?

19. What is the first line of *Dido's Lament* from Henry Purcell's opera *Dido and Aeneas*?

20. On which record label did Nigel Kennedy release his world-famous version of Vivaldi's *The Four Seasons*?

🎵 Round 4: Musical Colours

Complete the classical music titles by filling in the blanks with colours. But, be careful, there is one odd one out, just to confuse you ever so slightly.

1. *Brook _____ Suite* by Gustav Holst

2. *Rhapsody in _____* by George Gershwin

3. *The ___berg Variations* by J. S. Bach

4. *The _____ Poppy Suite* by Reinhold Gliere

5. *"When night her _____ veil"* by Henry Purcell

6. *The Banks of _____ Willow* by George Butterworth

7. *The ___ Boar* by Roger Quilter

8. *The _____ Bell* by Camille Saint-Saëns

9. *Farewell to Stromness* from *The _____ Cake Review* by Peter Maxwell Davies

10. *The _____ Symphony* by Arthur Bliss

11. *The ___ and _____ Waltz* by Franz Lehár

12. *_____ and Myrtle, here* by Robert Schumann

13. *The _____ Cockerel* by Rimsky-Korsakov

14. ___*beard's Castle* by Béla Bartók

15. *David of the* ___ *Rock* (Traditional)

16. *The* ___ *Swan* by Orlando Gibbons

17. *The* ___ *Knight* by Edward Elgar

18. *The* ___ *Bird* by Charles Villiers Stanford

19. *The* ___ *Cap* by Karl Ditters von Dittersdorf

20. *By the Beautiful* ___ *Danube* by Johann Strauss Jr

🔘 **Round 5:** The Year in Question

Each of these pairs (or trios) of musical and non-musical events took place in the same year in the 1700s. But what was the year in question? To help you, the answers are in chronological order — and the same year appears twice!

1. Antonio Vivaldi is ordained a priest in Venice. — Peter the Great founds St Petersburg.

2. George Frideric Handel's opera *Rinaldo* is performed at the Queen's Theatre in London. — *The Spectator* is founded in London.

3. George Frideric Handel's *Water Music* is performed on a barge on the River Thames. — England's first freemasonic Grand Lodge is founded in London.

4. The original Royal Academy of Music opens in London. — The "South Sea Bubble" bursts, leaving many investors penniless.

5. Johann Sebastian Bach's *St John Passion* is given its first performance in Leipzig. — Immanuel Kant is born.

6. George Frideric Handel becomes a naturalized British subject. — Sir Isaac Newton dies.

7. Johann Sebastian Bach's *St Matthew Passion* is given its first performance in its entirety in Leipzig. — The last execution for witchcraft in Britain takes place in Scotland.

8. Giovanni Battista Pergolesi finishes his best-known work, the *Stabat Mater*. — First recorded use of a bathing machine in an engraving by John Setterington.

9. Antonio Vivaldi gets into trouble with the Catholic Church because of his failure to say mass, and his close relationship with a young soprano. — The War of Jenkins' Ear begins between England and Spain.

10. Franz Joseph Haydn becomes a choirboy at the court chapel in Vienna. — Frederick the Great's reign begins in Prussia.

11. George Frideric Handel's *Messiah* receives its premiere. — Anders Celsius invents the centigrade thermometer.

12. George Frideric Handel has an operation on his eyes at Guy's Hospital in London. It is not a success. — Britain adopts the Gregorian calendar.

13. Wolfgang Amadeus Mozart is born in Salzburg. — More than 100 British soldiers die in the "Black Hole of Calcutta".

14. Aged 74, George Frideric Handel dies in London. — James Brindley designs the Worsley to Manchester Canal.

15. Wolfgang Amadeus Mozart gives his first concert in Italy, in the city of Verona. — James Hargreaves patents the spinning jenny.

16. Wolfgang Amadeus Mozart marries Constanze Weber in Vienna. — The hot-air balloon is invented by the Montgolfier brothers.

17. Wolfgang Amadeus Mozart's opera *The Marriage of Figaro* receives its premiere in Vienna. — Robert Burns's *Poems Chiefly in the Scottish Dialect* is published.

18. Niccolò Paganini makes his debut in Genoa. He is just 11 years old. — Slavery is abolished in the French colonies.

19. Franz Schubert and Gaetano Donizetti are born. — Samuel Taylor Coleridge's *Kubla Khan* is published.

20. Franz Joseph Haydn's *The Creation* is given its premiere in Vienna. — Napoleon becomes First Consul.

🏢 **Round 6:** Order! Order!

Johann Sebastian Bach had 20 children. Can you put them in the correct chronological birth order?

1. Carl Philipp Emanuel

2. Catherina Dorothea

3. Christian Gottlieb

4. Christiana Benedicta

5. Christiana Dorothea

6. Christiana Sophia Henrietta

7. Elisabeth Juliana Friederike

8. Ernst Andreas

9. Gottfried Heinrich

10. Johann August Abraham

11. Johann Christian

12. Johann Christoph

13. Johann Christoph Friedrich

14. Johann Gottfried Bernhard

15. Johanna Carolina

16. Leopold August

17. Maria Sophia

18. Regina Johanna

19. Regina Susanna

20. Wilhelm Friedemann

🎵 **Round 7:** Quick Fire (Easier)

1. Johann Sebastian Bach wrote two *Passions* named after which saints?

2. Johann Sebastian Bach believed that 14 was his own personal number. How did he arrive at this figure?

3. George Frideric Handel's father wasn't keen on him learning an instrument, so where did the boy's mother hide his harpsichord so that he could practise out of earshot?

4. George Frideric Handel's boss, the Elector of Hanover, eventually became the English monarch. What was his title?

5. Where is the body of George Frideric Handel buried?

6. Which Austrian town was the 18th-century composer Karl Ditters von Dittersdorf from?

7. For which nobleman did Wolfgang Amadeus Mozart's father work?

8. The film *Amadeus* suggests that Wolfgang Amadeus Mozart was murdered by which composer?

9. Just outside which city was Wolfgang Amadeus Mozart buried in an unmarked grave?

10. Which soprano is known as the "Doncaster Diva"?

11. Who was the first English composer to top the Classic FM Hall of Fame?

12. Where did Ludwig van Beethoven's ancestors originally come from?

13. What is the name of Ludwig van Beethoven's only opera?

14. Radio was born when Marconi successfully sent a message by wireless to a receiver over a mile away. During which period of classical music did this happen?

15. Nikolai Rimsky-Korsakov's family always expected him to go into a particular branch of the armed forces. Was it the army, navy or air force?

16. Upon which story is Nikolai Rimsky-Korsakov's greatest work, *Scheherazade*, based?

17. What nationality was the composer Bedřich Smetana?

18. Over what item of furnishing in the Savoy Theatre did W. S. Gilbert and Arthur Sullivan dramatically fall out?

19. Which city, home of Classic FM's orchestra in the north-west of England, was European Capital of Culture in 2008?

20. In which English county was Edward Elgar born?

// **Round 8:** True or False?

Decide whether each of these statements is true or false. But be warned: in an attempt to catch you out, some of the details have been changed only very slightly.

1. Ludwig van Beethoven liked to claim that the "van" in the middle of his name meant that he came from noble stock, but in fact he was descended from a perfectly ordinary family.

2. Niccolò Paganini would sometimes snap some of the strings of his violin mid-performance — and was still able to play brilliantly.

3. When Niccolò Paganini was a boy, his father would punish him for not practising his music, by withdrawing food and water.

4. The composer Charles-Valentin Alkan died after a shelfful of books fell on top of him.

5. The composer Ernest Chausson died after a cycling accident.

6. The composer Anton Webern died after being shot dead for unwittingly breaking an evening curfew not long after the end of the Second World War.

7. Some harps have pedals.

8. A piccolo is a large version of a flute.

9. A sackbut is an early version of a cello.

10. The last castrato, Alessandro Moreschi, was still singing at the Sistine Chapel in the Vatican until his retirement in 1973.

11. The real name of the soprano Maria Callas was Maria Kalogeropoulos.

12. The conductor Daniel Barenboim is also famous as a renowned cellist.

13. Felix Mendelssohn may have been famous for his *Scottish Symphony* and his *Hebrides Overture*, but he never actually set foot on Scottish soil.

14. Frédéric Chopin is best known for his compositions for the violin.

15. The woman who is regarded as the love of Frédéric Chopin's life often used to strut about the streets of Paris wearing men's clothes and smoking a large cigar.

16. Franz Liszt was very skilled at turning other people's big tunes into works for the piano. These included pieces by Beethoven, Berlioz, Rossini and Schubert.

17. Despite taking holy orders, Franz Liszt continued to enjoy a string of sexual conquests.

18. Mikhail Glinka's first job was as a civil servant in the Russian Ministry of Communications.

19. Alexander Borodin was the illegitimate son of a Georgian prince.

20. Despite coming from a wealthy background and having huge talent, both as a composer and as a pianist, Sergei Rachmaninov died in drink-induced poverty at the age of just 42.

🎵 **Round 9:** Quick Fire (Easier)

1. How is Edward Elgar's *Variations on an Original Theme* now better known?

2. Translate *"Nessun Dorma"* into English.

3. Which rock superstar had a hit in 2006 with an album of works by the 16th-century composer, singer and lutenist John Dowland?

4. The French composer Gabriel Fauré was given the option of two potential wives by a Parisienne matchmaker. How did he choose the lucky lady?

5. Give a word that rhymes with the correct pronunciation of Ralph Vaughan Williams's first name.

6. What is the name of the only piano work ever to top the Classic FM Hall of Fame?

7. At which London school was Gustav Holst the Director of Music for many years, even writing a suite dedicated to the place?

8. In which English city was Frederick Delius born?

9. What unusual event occurred at the premiere of Igor Stravinsky's ballet *The Rite of Spring*?

10. Sergei Prokofiev died on the same day as a Russian leader who had done an enormous amount to suppress his music. Who was that leader?

11. Francis Poulenc's father was a wealthy chemist who owned a pharmaceutical company. What was its name?

12. Which George Gershwin opera includes the hits "*Summertime*" and "*I got plenty o' Nuttin'*"?

13. Which legendary conductor changed his name from György Stern?

14. One of Dmitri Shostakovich's songs was sung over the radio back to mission control by which Russian cosmonaut?

15. What is the name of the work by John Cage that consists of around four-and-a-half minutes of silence?

16. John Tavener owes the release of his *Celtic Requiem* on Apple Records to which member of The Beatles?

17. In which building was the premiere performance of Paul McCartney's *Liverpool Oratorio* given?

18. What was the name of the choral work in four movements by Paul McCartney that received its premiere in the Royal Albert Hall in London at the end of 2006?

19. What was the name of the debut UK album by the New Zealand star Hayley Westenra?

20. What job did the tenor Alfie Boe do before he changed careers and became an opera singer?

𝄢 **Round 10:** Birthday Bonanza

Match the year of their birth to each composer:

John Barry, Béla Bartók, Georges Bizet, Alexander Borodin, Carl Philipp Emanuel Bach, Johann Christian Bach, Marc-Antoine Charpentier, Karl Ditters von Dittersdorf, Mikhail Glinka, George Frideric Handel, Karl Jenkins, Sergei Rachmaninov, Joaquín Rodrigo, Gioachino Rossini, Camille Saint-Saëns, Howard Shore, Johann Strauss Jr, Joby Talbot, Georg Philipp Telemann, Richard Wagner.

1. 1643

2. 1681

3. 1685

4. 1714

5. 1735

6. 1739

7. 1792

8. 1804

9. 1813

10. 1825

11. 1833

12. 1835

13. 1838

14. 1873

15. 1881

16. 1901

17. 1933

18. 1944

19. 1946

20. 1971

🎵 Round 11: Enigmas

These rounds are suitable for the more lateral thinker, so if you're the sort of person for whom the day is simply incomplete unless you've put yourself through the mental gymnastics of completing a crossword or two, then you should find our *Enigmas* particularly enjoyable. They have become a regular feature on Tim Lihoreau's *More Music Breakfast* programme every weekday morning between 6am and 9am on Classic FM.

Identify the classical music composer from the clues below. To help, we've included the number of letters in the answer in the brackets at the end of each clue.

1. Composer not all deaf. (2,5)

2. Is he the best composer in his? (5)

3. Composer? Rename him "A. Sullivan, wag". (7,8)

4. Blues is, I imagined, for composer. (8)

5. CIA shoots Kalashnikov's beginning, middle and end all out … for composer. (12)

6. Composer slips back in, in a gap. (8)

7. Composer's allure surrounds regional centre of excellence. (7)

8. NASA is sent to sort out composer. (5-5)

9. Heavenly body out much in sky for composer. (10)

10. Lindy dance, in C, gets composer all tangled up. (6)

🎼 **Round 12: They Said What?**

The greatest classical composers have never been backward in coming forward. Do you know which hallowed composers made each of these often not-so-hallowed utterances?

1. "It's easy to play any musical instrument: all you have to do is touch the right key at the right time and the instrument will play itself."

2. "One should try everything once, except incest and folk-dancing."

3. "Rossini would have been a great composer if his teacher had spanked him enough on the backside."

4. "If she can strike a low G or F like a death-rattle and a high F like the shriek of a little dog when you step on its tail, the house will resound with acclamations."

5. "I am not interested in having an orchestra sound like itself. I want it to sound like the composer."

6. "If there is anyone here whom I have not insulted, I beg his pardon."

7. "That old idea … of a composer suddenly having a terrific idea and sitting up all night to write it is nonsense. Night time is for sleeping."

8. "Listening to the Fifth Symphony of Ralph Vaughan Williams is like staring at a cow for 45 minutes."

9. "Never compose anything unless not composing it becomes a positive nuisance to you."

10. "Modern music is as dangerous as cocaine."

11. "I write as a sow piddles."

12. "I'm not handsome, but when women hear me play, they come crawling to my feet."

13. "A good conductor ought to be a good chauffeur. The qualities that make the one also make the other. They are concentration, an incessant control of attention, and presence of mind – the conductor only has to add a little sense of music."

14. "I'm told that Saint-Saëns has informed a delighted public that since the war began he has composed music for the stage, melodies, an elegy and a piece for the trombone. If he'd been making shell-cases instead it might have been all the better for music."

15. "Give me a laundry list and I will set it to music."

16. "In order to compose, all you have to do is think of a tune that nobody else has thought of."

17. "Pay no attention to what the critics say. No statue has ever been put up to a critic."

18. "Never look at the trombones, it only encourages them."

19. "Too many pieces of music finish too long after the end."

20. "Truly there would be reason to go mad if it were not for music."

Round 13: Mix & Match

Franz Joseph Haydn wrote a total of 104 symphonies. Many of them acquired nicknames. Can you match the number of each symphony with its nickname?

You can choose from:
The Bear, Clock, The Distracted, Drum Roll, Farewell, Fire, The Hen, The Hunt, Lamentation, London, Maria Theresa, Mercury, Military, Miracle, Oxford, The Passion, The Philosopher, The Queen, The Schoolmaster, Surprise.

1. No. 22 in E flat

2. No. 26 in D minor

3. No. 43 in E flat

4. No. 45 in F sharp minor

5. No. 48 in C

6. No. 49 in F minor

7. No. 55 in E flat

8. No. 59 in A

9. No. 60 in C

10. No. 73 in D

11. No. 82 in C

12. No. 83 in G minor

13. No. 85 in B flat

14. No. 92 in G

15. No. 94 in G

16. No. 96 in D

17. No. 100 in G

18. No. 101 in D

19. No. 103 in E flat

20. No. 104 in D

🎹 **Round 14:** Order! Order!

Put these musical speeds into the correct order, slowest to fastest:

1. Adagio

2. Andante

3. Allegretto

4. Allegro

5. Largo

6. Presto

Put these voices in the correct order, highest to lowest:

1. Baritone

2. Bass

3. Bass-baritone

4. Mezzo-soprano

5. Soprano

6. Tenor

Put these Masters of the King's or Queen's Music into the correct order, first to last:

1. Arnold Bax

2. Arthur Bliss

3. William Boyce

4. Edward Elgar

5. Nicholas Lanier

6. Peter Maxwell Davies

Put Mozart's Christian names in the correct order:

1. Amadeus

2. Chrysostomus

3. Johannes

4. Wolfgangus

🎵 **Round 15:** Mix & Match

Match the concert hall to the town or city.

You can choose from:
Aldeburgh, Amsterdam, Basingstoke, Belfast, Birmingham, Cardiff, Croydon, Edinburgh, Gateshead, Glasgow, Leipzig, Liverpool, London, Los Angeles, Manchester, New York, Poole, Vienna, Washington, Zurich.

   1. The Barbican

   2. The Philharmonic Hall

   3. Concertgebouw

   4. Carnegie Hall

   5. Walt Disney Concert Hall

   6. Usher Hall

   7. The Sage

   8. The Lighthouse

   9. St David's Hall

  10. The Bridgewater Hall

  11. Symphony Hall

  12. Musikverein

13. The Anvil

14. The Waterfront

15. Maltings Concert Hall

16. Gewandhaus

17. Tonhalle

18. Fairfield Halls

19. Kennedy Center

20. Royal Concert Hall

🔘 **Round 16:** The Year in Question

Each of these pairs (or trios) of musical and
non-musical events took place in the same year in the
1800s. But what was the year in question? To help you,
the answers are in chronological order.

1. Ludwig van Beethoven's *Symphony No. 1* is performed
   in Vienna. — Invention of the first chemical battery
   by Alessandro Volta.

2. Franz Liszt is born. — Jane Austen's *Sense and
   Sensibility* is published.

3. The Royal Philharmonic Society is founded in London.
   — Jane Austen's *Pride and Prejudice* is published.

4. Franz Schubert composes his first song using a text
   by Goethe. It's called *"Gretchen at the Spinning Wheel"*.
   — Stephenson designs his first steam locomotive,
   the Blucher.

5. Gioachino Rossini signs a contract to write *The Barber
   of Seville* in December. It will receive its premiere
   early in the following year. — Napoleon is defeated
   at the Battle of Waterloo.

6. Jacques Offenbach is born in Cologne. — The USA
   buys Florida from Spain.

7. Gioachino Rossini travels to England. He is welcomed
   by King George IV on a visit to Brighton. — Mexico is
   made a republic.

8. Richard Wagner writes his first complete opera. It's called *The Fairies*. — Slavery is outlawed in the British Empire.

9. Frédéric Chopin invents a new type of piano piece, the *Ballade*. — The first instalment of Charles Dickens's *Pickwick Papers* is published.

10. Max Bruch is born in Cologne and Georges Bizet is born in Paris. — Grace Darling and her father rescue nine people from the wreck of the *Forfarshire*.

11. Pyotr Ilyich Tchaikovsky is born in Russia and Niccolò Paganini dies in France. — Warren de la Rue passes an electric current through a coil in a vacuum tube and demonstrates the first electric light bulb.

12. The Vienna Philharmonic Orchestra is founded. — China hands over Hong Kong to Great Britain.

13. Felix Mendelssohn finishes his one and only *Violin Concerto*. — The first telegraph message is transmitted.

14. Richard Wagner's opera *Tannhäuser* gets its first performance in Dresden, but not everyone regards it as a big hit. — Dumas's *The Count of Monte Cristo* is published.

15. Robert Schumann's only *Piano Concerto* is given its debut performance in Leipzig. Clara Schumann is the soloist. — The sewing machine is patented.

16. Felix Mendelssohn conducts *Elijah* in London, Manchester and Birmingham, but tragedy strikes when his sister Fanny dies shortly afterwards. — The Brontë sisters are busy: Charlotte's *Jane Eyre* and Emily's *Wuthering Heights* are both published.

17. Hector Berlioz gives a concert in London on 29 June and Frédéric Chopin spends a few months in the city, giving a series of concerts, culminating in a performance on 16 November. — Ireland suffers from the potato famine, but California fares better: gold is discovered at Sutter's Mill and the Gold Rush is on.

18. Frédéric Chopin's *Funeral March* is played at his own funeral in Paris. — Charles Dickens's *David Copperfield* is published.

19. Giuseppe Verdi's opera *Il trovatore* receives its premiere in Rome and his *La traviata* gets its first public outing in Venice. — The first railway between New York and Chicago opens.

20. Robert Schumann attempts to commit suicide by throwing himself into the River Rhine. — The Charge of the Light Brigade takes place during the Crimean War.

🎼 **Round 17:** Famous Last Words

Can you match these musical people to their alleged famous last words?

1. "MOZART!"

2. "I shall hear in heaven!"

3. "But I have so little time."

4. "It is the end. Woe is me!"

5. "And I wish myself the joy of your fellowship at Whitsuntide."

6. "A thousand greetings to Balakirev!"

7. "I'm in a cold sweat. It is the sweat of death! How are you going to tell my father?"

8. "Gerda, I thank you for every day we've been together!"

9. "Doro … I can't get my breath!"

10. "Good little woman!"

11. "Swear to make them cut me open – so I won't be buried alive!"

12. "Now … I'll have eine kleine Pause!"

13. "Well, it must be so!"

14. "Now, I've finished with all earthly business, and high time too: yes, my dear child, now comes death."

15. "I'll say no more about it, and leave the description of the festivities to the more expert pen of other correspondents!"

16. "Sinner, thou must die!"

17. "Weary, very weary."

18. "I obtained three days delay, that I might commend myself and all these to thy beatitude, and that thou might consecrate this my house as a church."

19. "I'm tiring of ruling over slaves. We are over the mountain – we shall go better now."

20. "Did I not tell you I was writing this for myself?"

🎵 **Round 18:** Whose Aria Is It Anyway?

From which opera is each of these famous arias or choruses taken?

1. *"Celeste Aida"*

2. *"Largo al factotum"*

3. *"O soave fanciulla"*

4. *"Toreador Song"*

5. *"The Flower Duet"*

6. *"Voi che sapete"*

7. *"Chorus of the Hebrew Slaves"*

8. *"Au fond du temple saint"*

9. *"When I am laid in earth"*

10. *"Sempre Libera"*

11. *"The Willow Song"*

12. *"Song to the Moon"*

13. *"Casta Diva"*

14. *"Nessun Dorma"*

15. *"Là ci darem la mano"*

16. *"O welche Lust"*

17. *"O mio babbino caro"*

18. *"Easter Hymn"*

19. *"Vissi d'arte"*

20. *"It ain't necessarily so"*

Round 19: Definitive Mix & Match

Match the musical term to its definition. You can choose from:

a capella, adagio, allegro, aria, cadenza, chamber music, concerto, gavotte, intermezzo, legato, libretto, Lied, Kapellmeister, movement, opus, oratorio, quartet, quintet, toccata, trio.

1. A piece of music written for three players.

2. A religious work featuring soloists, a choir and orchestra. Sometimes acted out, but usually without scenery or costumes.

3. Unaccompanied choral singing.

4. A piece of music written for five players.

5. The Italian instruction from a composer to a performer to play the music in a lively and bright way.

6. A piece of music written for keyboard, where the performer will often have to play both very quickly and very delicately.

7. A solo song from an opera.

8. Music that was originally designed to be played by small instrumental groups in people's homes rather than in churches or concert halls.

9. An orchestral piece that usually features a starring role for the player of one particular instrument, who sits out at the front of the stage, next to the conductor.

10. An old French dance.

11. The Italian instruction from a composer to a performer to play the music smoothly.

12. The words of an opera.

13. The music director of a nobleman's choir.

14. A piece of music written for four players.

15. An individual section of a bigger work such as a concerto or a symphony.

16. An instrumental interlude in the middle of an opera, used to show that time has passed by between two bits of action on stage.

17. Often used as the name of the slow movement of a classical work.

18. A musical work, often followed by a number for cataloguing purposes.

19. An improvised section, usually towards the end of a work, which gives the soloist a chance to show off.

20. A type of German solo song, often performed with a piano as accompaniment.

◯ **Round 20:** Name that Composer

Each of the groups of works below was written by one person. Can you name that composer?

1. *Abdelazer, Trumpet Tune and Air in D, Come Ye Sons of Art*

2. *The Four Seasons, Gloria, "Nulla in Mundo Pax Sincera"*

3. *Brandenburg Concertos, Goldberg Variations, Toccata and Fugue in D minor*

4. *Water Music, Solomon, Xerxes*

5. *The Creation, The Seasons, Symphony No. 94 ("Surprise")*

6. *Laudate Dominum, Requiem, Clarinet Concerto in A*

7. *Fidelio, Für Elise, Moonlight Sonata*

8. *Marche Militaire No. 1, Piano Quintet ("Trout"), Rosamunde*

9. *Symphonie fantastique, The Childhood of Christ, Requiem*

10. *O for the Wings of a Dove, Songs without Words, A Midsummer Night's Dream*

11. *Nocturne No. 2; Prelude No. 15 ("Raindrop"), Waltz No. 6 ("Minute" Waltz)*

12. *Scenes from Childhood No. 7 – Dreaming, Fantasie in C, Dichterliebe*

13. *Hungarian Rhapsody No. 2, Liebestraum No. 3, Rhapsodie espagnole*

14. *The Pearl Fishers, L'Arlésienne Suite No. 1, Jeux d'enfants*

15. *A Life for the Tsar, Ruslan and Ludmila, Kamarinskaya*

16. *Prince Igor, In the Steppes of Central Asia, String Quartet No. 2*

17. *Night on the Bare Mountain, Pictures at an Exhibition, Boris Godunov*

18. *Scheherazade, Flight of the Bumblebee, Capriccio Espagnol*

19. *The Nutcracker, 1812 Overture, Swan Lake*

20. *Rusalka, Serenade for Strings, Slavonic Dances*

🎵 **Round 21:** Quick Fire (Intermediate)

1. Which animal does the double-bass represent in the *Carnival of the Animals* by Camille Saint-Saëns?

2. Who wrote the music to the children's classic *Babar the Elephant*?

3. Edvard Grieg wrote his *Peer Gynt Suite* as the incidental music to a play of the same name by which Norwegian writer?

4. Which Irish composer is said to have invented the nocturne?

5. What does cor anglais translate as?

6. The late Jack Brymer was the principal clarinettist with which orchestra from 1971 until his retirement?

7. The Prince of Wales has recently reintroduced the tradition of having a harpist as a member of his court. What was the name of the first person he appointed to this position?

8. What was the name of the Belgian who invented the saxophone?

9. Legend has it that Johann Sebastian Bach walked four hundred or so kilometres to hear which organist play?

10. Which English orchestra had the composer Max Bruch as its principal conductor for three years?

11. Which great movie composer plays the piano on the soundtrack to the 1961 film *Breakfast at Tiffany's*?

12. In Frederick Delius's opera *A Village Romeo and Juliet*, the characters take a *Walk to the Paradise Garden*. What exactly was the Paradise Garden?

13. Edward Elgar wrote the music, but who wrote the words to "*Land of Hope and Glory*"?

14. The composers Domenico Scarlatti and George Frideric Handel once had a duel. Handel was on the organ, while Scarlatti played the harpsichord. Who won?

15. The national anthem for which European country is based on music written by Franz Joseph Haydn?

16. Aled Jones became famous for singing "*Walking in the Air*" from *The Snowman*. Who composed the song?

17. The *Can-Can* comes from which operetta by Jacques Offenbach?

18. Henry Purcell was the organist at which English abbey?

19. Benjamin Britten borrowed the theme from Henry Purcell's *Rondeau* from *Abdelazar* to use as the basis for his most famous piece for children. What is its name?

20. What was a "Schubertiad"?

🔒 Round 22: Enigmas

Solve the cryptic crossword-style clues to identify each of these composers.

1. Composer, Beethoven's chum, melts when 100 tenor saxes leave. (6)

2. Composer's apple centre gets back sick? (7)

3. The enigma of Nimrod, rigorously sought, is a composer's name! (7)

4. Initially polyphonic art composer. (4)

5. Tenor Alfie hangs around yacht club for composer (5)

6. Composer locked up in clinic cupboard (7)

7. Composer grew an aberration? (6)

8. Composer's got talent? (7)

9. NB: Entries for composer? (9)

10. Composer's fabrication is wrapped in Indian garment (7)

⚬ **Round 23: Cinematic Sounds**

1. Which English composer won an Oscar for his soundtrack to *The Bridge on the River Kwai*?

2. Who wrote the *Organ Symphony* made famous to a whole new generation of listeners by Babe, the pig that thought it was a sheepdog?

3. Oliver Stone notably used which famous piece by Samuel Barber in his Vietnam War film *Platoon*?

4. What is the name of the film that saw the first collaboration between the composer John Williams and the director Steven Spielberg?

5. What was the name of the Ken Russell film about the life of the English composer Frederick Delius?

6. Who played Gustav Mahler in Ken Russell's 1974 film about the great man?

7. Modest Mussorgsky's *Night on a Bare Mountain* was used in which Walt Disney cartoon?

8. The film *Amadeus*, about the life of Wolfgang Amadeus Mozart, was directed by Milos Forman. But on whose stage play was it based?

9. Joaquín Rodrigo's *Concierto de Aranjuez* was referred to as "Concerto de Orange Juice" in which film about a northern mining town?

10. What was the name of the 1908 film for which Camille Saint-Saëns composed the first ever film soundtrack?

11. Which work by George Frideric Handel was used as the theme music to *The Madness of King George*?

12. Who directed the film *2001: A Space Odyssey*, which used Richard Strauss's *Also sprach Zarathustra* in its opening?

13. The great film composer Erich Korngold became an American citizen in 1943, but what nationality was he originally?

14. For which studio symphony orchestra was Bernard Herrmann the Chief Conductor between 1942 and 1959?

15. From 1924 to 1925, a silent film was produced of one of Richard Strauss's operas, making a significant advance in the relationship between music and cinema in the process. Which opera was it?

16. Which Scottish composer worked with the director Baz Luhrmann on his films *Romeo and Juliet* and *Moulin Rouge!*?

17. At which British music college did the composer of the soundtrack to *Titanic*, James Horner, train?

18. What was the name of the 1998 film about the relationship between the cellist Jacqueline du Pré and her sister Hilary?

19. Who composed the music for *Citizen Kane* and *Psycho*?

20. For which film was Arnold Schoenberg's *Accompaniment to a Film Scene* written?

🎵 **Round 24:** Quick Fire (Intermediate)

1. What is the name of the style of singing where the composer writes several separate tunes for people with different voices, which combine together harmoniously?

2. Who wrote the 1970 opera *Taverner*, about the life of the early English composer John Taverner?

3. The composer Thomas Tallis wrote music for two Queens of England. One was Catholic and one was Protestant. Who were they?

4. The early music composer Thomas Tallis was a lay clerk at which English cathedral?

5. With whom did the composer William Byrd operate a jobshare for around 40 years as the composer and organist to the Chapel Royal?

6. The early music composer William Byrd was the organist and choirmaster at which cathedral between 1563 and 1572?

7. Elizabeth I jointly granted the composers William Byrd and Thomas Tallis a patent allowing them the monopoly on what in England for 21 years from 1575?

8. Jacopo Peri is the man to whom history has given the credit for writing the world's first opera. His first operatic work was called *Dafne*, but what was the name of his second work?

9. For which French king was Jean-Baptiste Lully the personal composer?

10. By the time he was ten, Henry Purcell was a choirboy in which choir?

11. In Purcell's opera *Dido and Aeneas*, Dido is queen of where?

12. What was the first piece of music played on Classic FM?

13. Which work was number one in the first Classic FM Hall of Fame back in 1996?

14. Vivaldi was excused having to say mass because he claimed to suffer from which illness?

15. Between Johann Sebastian Bach leaving school and becoming an organist, which instrument did he make money from playing?

16. Johann Sebastian Bach's first wife, Maria Barbara, was already related to him in what way?

17. When Handel was eight years old a nobleman heard him play and was so impressed that he ensured the boy had lessons. What was the nobleman's name?

18. At the court of which German nobleman was Handel given a job?

19. *"Zadok the Priest"* was written by George Frideric Handel as a coronation anthem for which English monarch?

20. In which European city was George Frideric Handel's *Messiah* given its premiere in 1742?

// **Round 25:** True or False?

Decide whether each of these statements is true or false. But be warned: in an attempt to catch you out, some of the details have been changed only very slightly.

1. Ludwig van Beethoven, Franz Schubert and Gustav Mahler each wrote 12 symphonies.

2. Cello is actually short for Violoncello.

3. Every child at school in Belgium is required by law to learn to play the harmonica.

4. Ludwig van Beethoven was the first composer to use a trombone in a symphony.

5. Johann Sebastian Bach wrote a cantata about fizzy water.

6. Johann Sebastian Bach's *Air on the G String* wasn't actually written to be played on the G string at all.

7. The father of film composer John Barry ran a cinema.

8. Ludwig van Beethoven never actually gave the nickname *Moonlight Sonata* to his *Sonata No. 14 in C sharp minor*.

9. Carmen, the heroine in Bizet's eponymous opera, worked in a hosiery factory.

10. Alexander Borodin's first published work was called
*On the Action of Ethyl Iodide on Hydrobenzamide and
Amarine.*

11. Johannes Brahms used to play piano in brothels as a
way of earning his keep.

12. Although Aaron Copland was American, both his
parents were originally German.

13. Peter Maxwell Davies wrote his *Farewell to Stromness*
to be played as a ship bearing the name *Stromness*
left port.

14. Claude Debussy finished off his big hit *La Mer* when
he was beside the seaside in Bridlington.

15. Antonín Dvořák was a trainspotter.

16. George Gershwin once wrote a song called *"I'm a
poached egg!"*

17. During the First World War, the French composer
Maurice Ravel was a taxi driver.

18. Nikolai Rimsky-Korsakov partially wrote his *Symphony
in E flat* while stationed just off the coast at Bridlington.

19. Charles Darwin was the grandfather of Ralph
Vaughan Williams.

20. The film soundtrack composer Hans Zimmer also
wrote the theme tune for Henry Kelly's long-running
daytime television quiz show, *Going For Gold.*

🎵 Round 26: Quick Fire (Intermediate)

1. Christoph Willibald Gluck's *The Dance of the Blessed Spirits* comes from a ballet section of which of his operas?

2. What is the name of the family who were musical patrons to Franz Joseph Haydn throughout his career?

3. Which member of the Bach family is sometimes referred to as "the London Bach"?

4. How many quintets did Luigi Boccherini compose for various combinations of instruments?

5. During his lifetime, the composer Luigi Boccherini toured Italy, France and Spain as a virtuoso performer on which instrument?

6. By what nickname was Wolfgang Amadeus Mozart's sister Maria Anna known?

7. Wolfgang Amadeus Mozart went on his first tour of Europe when he was six years old. It took in Munich, Vienna, Paris, London and Amsterdam. For how many years did it last?

8. According to legend, on hearing which popular work in Italy did the young Wolfgang Amadeus Mozart rush off and scribble down the whole work onto manuscript paper, note perfect?

9. What was the name of Wolfgang Amadeus Mozart's wife?

10. How old was Wolfgang Amadeus Mozart when he died?

11. Which operetta composer also wrote the tune to the hymn *"Onward, Christian Soldiers"*?

12. Which other famous composer did Ludwig van Beethoven describe as being a teacher "from whom I learned absolutely nothing"?

13. Which other famous composer, when he was a boy, played for Wolfgang Amadeus Mozart, impressing the older man enough for him to say: "Keep your eye on him; one day he will make the world talk of him"?

14. What is the composer Louis Spohr said to have invented some time around 1820, for which violinists ever since have had cause to thank him?

15. After Niccolò Paganini died, why did the Church initially refuse to allow his body to be buried on its land?

16. Franz Schubert contracted syphilis in 1823, but it was another disease that claimed his life five years later. What was it?

17. For which profession did Hector Berlioz begin training in Paris, before switching to music?

18. How many brass bands did Hector Berlioz include in the score for his *Requiem*?

19. A Welsh male voice choir stormed the charts in 2006, with their album becoming the best-selling classical disc of the year. What is their name?

20. The album back-catalogue of which Scottish violinist includes *Fantasie*, *Italia* and *The Silver Violin*?

🔘 **Round 27:** The Year in Question

Each of these pairs (or trios) of musical and non-musical events took place in the same year in the 1800s and 1900s. But what was the year in question? To help you, the answers are in chronological order.

1. Jacques Offenbach scandalizes polite society in Paris with the first performance of his *Orpheus in the Underworld*, which includes the *Can-Can*. — The Suez Canal Company is formed.

2. Richard Wagner finishes composing his opera *Tristan und Isolde*. — Charles Darwin's *On the Origin of the Species* is published.

3. Frederick Delius is born in England and Claude Debussy is born in France. — Victor Hugo's *Les Misérables* is published.

4. Anton Bruckner finishes his *Symphony Number 0*. — Tolstoy's *War and Peace* is published.

5. Carl Nielsen is born in Denmark; Alexander Glazunov is born in Russia and Jean Sibelius is born in Finland. — Abraham Lincoln is assassinated.

6. *Coppélia*, a ballet composed by Léo Delibes, gets its premiere in Paris. — Rome is made the capital city of Italy.

7. Richard Wagner's mighty opera cycle *The Ring* receives its first complete performance in Bayreuth. — Alexander Graham Bell invents the telephone.

8. Pyotr Ilyich Tchaikovsky's *Swan Lake* receives its first performance at the Bolshoi Theatre in Moscow. – Thomas Edison invents the phonograph.

9. Antonín Dvořák becomes a star following the publication of his *Slavonic Dances*. – David Hughes invents the microphone.

10. The first, four-volume, edition of George Grove's *Dictionary of Music and Musicians* is published. – The University of London becomes the first in the UK to admit women on equal terms with men.

11. The Boston Symphony Orchestra is founded. – Tsar Alexander II is assassinated.

12. The Berlin Philharmonic Orchestra is founded. – Tuberculosis germs are identified by Robert Koch.

13. The Metropolitan Opera is founded in New York. – Robert Louis Stevenson's *Treasure Island* is published.

14. Sergei Rachmaninov finishes composing his *Piano Concerto No. 1*, while he is still a student at the Moscow Conservatoire. – Sir Arthur Conan Doyle's *The Adventures of Sherlock Holmes* is published.

15. Claude Debussy's *Prélude à l'après-midi d'un faune* is given its first performance in Paris. – Rudyard Kipling's *Jungle Book* is published.

16. Giacomo Puccini's opera *La Bohème* gets its debut in Turin, under the baton of the great Arturo Toscanini. – The first modern Olympic Games take place.

17. George Gershwin is born. – H. G. Wells's *The War of the Worlds* is published.

18. Edward Elgar finishes composing his *Enigma Variations*. – Valdemar Poulsen demonstrates the principle of magnetic tape recording.

19. Birmingham is the venue for the premiere of *The Dream of Gerontius* by Edward Elgar. – Joseph Conrad's *Lord Jim* is published.

20. Giuseppe Verdi dies in Milan. – The first wireless telegraphic signals are sent across the Atlantic by Marconi.

🎼 **Round 28:** In Good Voice

All of these singing stars are sopranos, mezzo-sopranos, countertenors, tenors, baritones, bass-baritones or basses, but who is which?

1. Roberto Alagna

2. Marcelo Álvarez

3. Cecilia Bartoli

4. Alfie Boe

5. James Bowman

6. Maria Callas

7. José Carreras

8. Plácido Domingo

9. Renée Fleming

10. Lesley Garrett

11. Angela Gheorghiu

12. Katherine Jenkins

13. Emma Kirkby

14. Natasha Marsh

15. Anna Netrebko

16. Anne Sofie von Otter

17. Luciano Pavarotti

18. Andreas Scholl

19. Bryn Terfel

20. John Tomlinson

🎵 **Round 29:** Quick Fire (Intermediate)

1. The conductor Hans von Bülow came up with the name "The Three Bs" to describe a trio of composing greats. Who were they?

2. How many strings does a violin have?

3. In the first ten years of the annual listeners' poll, the Classic FM Hall of Fame, which opera consistently achieved the highest position in the chart?

4. Even though he spent 17 years working on it, Alexander Borodin didn't complete his opera *Prince Igor*. Which friend finished it off for him?

5. What did Pyotr Ilyich Tchaikovsky study at university?

6. Although there is a school of thought that he deliberately took his own life, what was the official reason given for Pyotr Ilyich Tchaikovsky's death?

7. What is the English translation of Bedřich Smetana's best-known work, *Má Vlast*?

8. Of which two forms of transport was Antonín Dvořák a particularly big fan?

9. What were the first two names of W. S. Gilbert (of Gilbert & Sullivan fame)?

10. In which opera by Jacques Offenbach does the *Barcarolle* feature?

11. For which two famous French composers – both of whose names start with the letter "B" – did Léo Delibes work as chorus master at Paris's Théâtre Lyrique?

12. What sort of shop did Edward Elgar's father own during the composer's childhood?

13. What was the name of Giacomo Puccini's final unfinished opera?

14. Which of Gustav Mahler's symphonies is known as "The Symphony of a Thousand"?

15. Who said of Sergei Rachmaninov: "[His] immortalizing totality was his scowl. He was a six-and-a-half-foot-tall scowl … he was an awesome man"?

16. Ravel, Fauré and Rachmaninov all wrote one each, while Vaughan Williams wrote three wordless songs. What are they better known as?

17. At which music college did Ralph Vaughan Williams and Gustav Holst study together?

18. Gustav Holst was of Swedish descent, but in which English county was he born?

19. To distract him from composing, Frederick Delius's father sent him to run what sort of business in America?

20. Which two famous composers criss-crossed Hungary, gathering recordings of authentic Hungarian folk tunes on a primitive recording machine which imprinted the sounds on wax cylinders?

🎵 **Round 30:** Mix & Match

Match the famous composer to their big hit:

You can choose from:
Johann Sebastian Bach, Ludwig van Beethoven, Georges Bizet, George Butterworth, Aaron Copland, Peter Maxwell Davies, Edward Elgar, George Gershwin, George Frideric Handel, Karl Jenkins, Pietro Mascagni, Modest Mussorgsky, Sergei Rachmaninov, Jean Sibelius, Bedřich Smetana, Igor Stravinsky, Pyotr Ilyich Tchaikovsky, Ralph Vaughan Williams, Antonio Vivaldi, William Walton.

1. *The Lark Ascending*

2. *The Enigma Variations*

3. *The Armed Man (A Mass for Peace)*

4. *Finlandia*

5. *1812 Overture*

6. *Má Vlast*

7. *The Pearl Fishers*

8. *Rhapsody on a Theme of Paganini*

9. *Rhapsody in Blue*

10. *Cavalleria rusticana*

11. *The Four Seasons*

12. *The Banks of Green Willow*

13. *Toccata and Fugue in D minor*

14. *Pictures at an Exhibition*

15. *Egmont Overture*

16. *Farewell to Stromness*

17. *Sarabande*

18. *The Rite of Spring*

19. *Crown Imperial*

20. *Appalachian Spring*

🎵 **Round 31:** Quick Fire (Intermediate)

1. Which great Russian impresario commissioned Igor Stravinsky to write the ballets *The Firebird* and *Petrushka*?

2. Which fruit was included in the title of an opera by Sergei Prokofiev?

3. Sibelius's *Andante festivo* was written for the 25th anniversary of what sort of Finnish industrial plant?

4. In 1948, William Walton left Britain and moved to which island off the Italian coast?

5. Which of Dmitri Shostakovich's symphonies has the subtitle "*A Soviet Artist's Practical Creative Reply to Just Criticism*?"

6. The American composer John Cage inserted pieces of metal and rubber into the body of a piano to create a variation on the instrument. What was this known as?

7. Benjamin Britten's *War Requiem* was written for the opening of which cathedral?

8. Which composer ran a piano shop on 195 Tottenham Court Road in London?

9. Of which American orchestra was Leonard Bernstein the music director between 1958 and 1969?

10. Peter Maxwell Davies and Harrison Birtwistle both studied at the Royal Manchester College of Music, as part of a group of young British composers. What were they collectively known as?

11. Which soprano featured on a hit recording of Henryk Górecki's *Symphony of Sorrowful Songs* with the London Sinfonietta in the early 1990s?

12. In 1969, Arvo Pärt stopped composing after becoming a member of which religious group?

13. John Tavener's work, *The Protecting Veil*, was written for which cellist?

14. The composers Philip Glass, Steve Reich and Terry Riley are all exponents of a deceptively simple style of music, which often features a few notes repeated over and over again. What is it called?

15. Who was the first composer to be made a life peer?

16. What was the name given to the group of French composers Georges Auric, Louis Durey, Arthur Honegger, Darius Milhaud, Francis Poulenc and Germaine Tailleferre?

17. Where in Oxford was William Walton a boy chorister?

18. Sergei Prokofiev and Dmitri Shostakovich both studied at which Russian music college?

19. In musical circles, what does the acronym FRWCMD stand for?

20. What is the name of the young Russian who took over as the Royal Liverpool Philharmonic Orchestra's Principal Conductor in 2006?

Round 32: True or False?

Decide whether each of these statements is true or false. But be warned: in an attempt to catch you out, some of the details have been changed only very slightly.

1. The Catholic Church made the composer-nun Hildegard of Bingen a saint.

2. The Italian composer Giovanni Pierluigi da Palestrina's surname wasn't really Palestrina. Palestrina was, in fact, his home town.

3. Pope Marcellus, the dedicatee of Palestrina's *Missa Papae Marcelli*, was dead by the time the composer had finished it.

4. The Chapel Royal is not actually a place, but is instead a group of singers.

5. Jean-Baptiste Lully made his name in France, but was originally Italian.

6. Georg Philipp Telemann composed around 9,700 works.

7. After he died, it took 46 years to collect and publish all of Johann Sebastian Bach's works.

8. Christoph Willibald Gluck died in Vienna after suffering a series of strokes brought on by his insistence on drinking an after-dinner liqueur against his doctor's wishes.

9. Franz Joseph Haydn very nearly became a castrato, on the advice of his choirmaster, until the boy's father found out and told him what had to happen to him to allow his high voice to remain.

10. By the time he was 12, Wolfgang Amadeus Mozart had already completed seven operas.

11. Edvard Grieg's great-grandfather emigrated to Australia after the Battle of Culloden.

12. As a youngster, the Spanish composer Isaac Albéniz used to perform a party trick where he would stand dressed as a musketeer with the piano keyboard behind him, playing tunes with the backs of his hands.

13. Anton Bruckner graduated from a correspondence course on music composition at the age of 10.

14. *The Four Last Songs* was the last work that Richard Strauss wrote before he died.

15. The composer who wrote *Finlandia* was actually French.

16. When Sergei Rachmaninov moved from Russia to America, he built himself a new home that was absolutely identical to the one he had left behind in Moscow.

17. One of Erik Satie's strangest compositions is called *Vexations*. It is made up of the same few bars of music, which are played over and over again a total of 840 times.

18. Erik Satie's ballet *Parade* features parts for typewriter, whistle, lawnmower, knitting needles and siren.

19. Tortoises, an elephant, kangaroos, donkeys and gerbils all feature in Camille Saint-Saëns's *Carnival of the Animals*.

20. The chart-topping mezzo-soprano Katherine Jenkins was born in Skegness.

⬛ **Round 33:** Enigmas

Solve the cryptic crossword-style clues to identify each of these composers.

1. Tram's return takes in magical land for composer (6)

2. Composer's banking brother misses out on Handel's first in a decade (8)

3. Composer found Kismet an advantage (7)

4. Withdrawal to nice island for composer? (6)

5. Composer's trial cast needs revamping (9)

6. Composer holed up in laundry basket (4)

7. Heal badly with a short man around to get composer. (6)

8. Middlesborough FC's noise finds composer. (7)

9. Bookstall is where to find composer (6)

10. New Salop is upset losing county composer (5)

🎼 Round 34: On the Box

Classical music has long been used to help sell all sorts of products in television commercials. Can you match the ten pieces below to the ten products or brands?

You can choose from:
British Airways, Cadbury Fruit & Nut, De Beers diamonds, Hamlet cigars, Hovis bread, John Lewis, Levi jeans, Lloyds TSB, Old Spice, Orange.

1. Pyotr Ilyich Tchaikovsky: *Dance of the Reed-Flutes* from *The Nutcracker*

2. Carl Orff: "*O Fortuna*" from *Carmina Burana*

3. Karl Jenkins: *Palladio*

4. Léo Delibes: *Flower Duet* from *Lakmé*

5. Johann Sebastian Bach: *Air on a G String*

6. Antonín Dvořák: *Symphony No. 9*

7. George Frideric Handel: *Sarabande*

8. John Tavener: *The Lamb*

9. Elena Kats-Chernin: *Eliza's Aria*

10. Ludovico Einaudi: *Le Onde*

It's not just advertisers who have plundered the classical music back-catalogue for great music. The people who make the programmes between the ad breaks have done the same thing over the years. Match these ten classical works to the ten television programmes to which they provided the signature tune.

You can choose from:
Alfred Hitchcock Presents …, *The* (American) *Civil War*, *The Eurovision Song Contest*, *Horse of the Year Show*, *The Lone Ranger*, *Monty Python's Flying Circus*, *The Onedin Line*, *The Sky at Night*, *The South Bank Show*, *What the Papers Say*.

11. Malcolm Arnold: *English Dance No. 5*

12. Marc-Antoine Charpentier: *Te Deum*

13. Charles Gounod: *Funeral March of a Marionette*

14. Aram Khachaturian: *Adagio of Spartacus and Phrygia*

15. Wolfgang Amadeus Mozart: *A Musical Joke*

16. Sergei Rachmaninov: *Variations on a Theme of Paganini*

17. Gioachino Rossini: *William Tell Overture*

18. John Philip Sousa: *The Liberty Bell*

19. Jean Sibelius: *At the Castle Gate* from *Pelléas and Mélisande*

20. Jay Ungar: *Ashokan Farewell*

🎹 **Round 35:** Order! Order!

Put these musical instrument formations in the correct
order, starting with the one involving the smallest
number of musicians:

1. Decimet

2. Duet

3. Nonet

4. Octet

5. Quartet

6. Quintet

7. Septet

8. Solo

9. Sextet

10. Trio

Put these string instruments in order of size, starting
with the smallest:

1. Cello

2. Double-bass

3. Viola

4. Violin

Put these operas in the order in which they were premiered:

1. Christoph Willibald Gluck: *Orpheus and Eurydice*

2. Claudio Monteverdi: *La favola d'Orfeo*

3. Georges Bizet: *Carmen*

4. Giacomo Puccini: *Madame Butterfly*

5. Giuseppe Verdi: *Otello*

6. Jacques Offenbach: *Orpheus in the Underworld*

Round 36: Quick Fire (Fiendish)

1. Which is the lowest woodwind instrument of the orchestra?

2. Composer Richard Strauss's father was a horn player who performed a number of premieres for – and was consulted by – which famous German opera composer?

3. It's now virtually disappeared from the musical landscape, but what sort of instrument is a heckelphone?

4. The jazz saxophonist Jan Garbarek worked with which group of singers on his album *Officium*, which includes the big Classic FM hit *"Parce mihi Domine"*?

5. Which Italian professor pieced together Tomaso Albinoni's *Adagio for Strings* and probably deserves most of the credit for actually writing it?

6. Which fellow famous composer was a torch-bearer at the funeral of Ludwig van Beethoven?

7. What was the name of the Irish actress with whom the French composer Hector Berlioz fell passionately in love, eventually marrying her in 1833?

8. Johannes Brahms wrote his *Academic Festival Overture* when he was given an honorary degree from which university?

9. Anton Bruckner is buried under the organ at a monastery in which city?

10. Frédéric Chopin had a passionate affair with the novelist George Sand. But this was her nom de plume; what was her real name?

11. What is the enigma in Edward Elgar's *Enigma Variations*?

12. Can you name the five composers who together made up "The Mighty Handful"?

13. How many days did Gioachino Rossini claim it took him to write *The Barber of Seville* in its entirety?

14. Camille Saint-Saëns was a clever chap and developed a very keen interest in lepidoptery. What is this the study of?

15. For which orchestra did Jean Sibelius fail his audition as a violinist in 1891?

16. Pyotr Ilyich Tchaikovsky received an honorary degree from Cambridge University in 1893, but there were two other composers there picking up gongs on the same day. Who were they?

17. Which record label is home to Tine Thing Helseth and Alison Balsom – two of the most famous female trumpeters of the present time?

18. What is antiphonal singing?

19. What is the name of the monk who published his theories on musical notation in around 1025, and who is now usually given the credit for inventing the writing down of music?

20. Hildegard of Bingen wasn't really born in Bingen itself. Where was she actually from?

🎼 **Round 37: They Come from Where?**

Match the famous composers to the country of their birth.

You can choose from:
Armenia, Austria, Belgium, Canada, England, Estonia, Finland, France, Germany, Hungary, Italy, Norway, Poland, Russia, Scotland, Spain, USA, Wales.

1. Frederick Delius

2. Arvo Pärt

3. Zbigniew Preisner

4. Franz Joseph Haydn

5. Louis Spohr

6. Hector Berlioz

7. Franz Liszt

8. Edvard Grieg

9. Isaac Albéniz

10. Arthur Sullivan

11. Jean Sibelius

12. Sergei Rachmaninov

13. George Gershwin

14. Karl Jenkins

15. Howard Shore

16. Aram Khachaturian

17. James MacMillan

18. Patrick Doyle

19. Guillaume Dufay

20. Domenico Zipoli

🎵 **Round 38: Name that Composer**

Each of the groups of works listed below was written by one person. Can you name that composer?

1. *Holberg Suite, Peer Gynt Suite, Lyric Pieces*

2. *The Mikado, Ivanhoe, Symphony in E*

3. *Lakmé, Coppélia, Sylvia*

4. *By the Beautiful Blue Danube, Tales from the Vienna Woods, Thunder and Lightning Polka*

5. *Aida, La forza del destino, La traviata*

6. *The Flying Dutchman, Lohengrin, Tristan and Isolde*

7. *Academic Festival Overture, Hungarian Dance No. 5, Violin Concerto*

8. *Violin Concerto No. 1 in G minor, Kol Nidrei, Scottish Fantasy*

9. *The Carnival of the Animals, Danse macabre, "Organ" Symphony No. 3*

10. *Cantique de Jean Racine, Dolly Suite, Clair de lune*

11. *Enigma Variations, Chanson de Matin, Salut d'Amour*

12. *La Bohème, Gianni Schicchi, Madame Butterfly*

13. *Also sprach Zarathustra, Der Rosenkavalier, Four Last Songs*

14. *Karelia Suite, The Swan of Tuonela, Valse triste*

15. *Vocalise, Rhapsody on a Theme of Paganini, Aleko*

16. *Clair de lune, La Mer, Prélude à L'Après-midi d'un faune*

17. *Le Tombeau de Couperin, Pavane pour une infante défunte, Daphnis and Chloé*

18. *Fantasia on a Theme of Thomas Tallis, The Lark Ascending, English Folk Song Suite*

19. *La Calinda, On Hearing the First Cuckoo in Spring, The Walk to the Paradise Garden*

20. *Romeo and Juliet, Lieutenant Kijé Suite, The Love for Three Oranges*

🎵 **Round 39:** Quick Fire (Fiendish)

1. Guillaume de Machaut was one of the "Ars Nova" composers of the 1300s. What does that translate as?

2. Guillaume de Machaut became a canon in which French city around the age of 40?

3. In which cathedral did the Belgian composer Guillaume Dufay begin his career as a boy chorister?

4. The early music composer Thomas Tallis was an organist at which Essex abbey?

5. Elizabeth I granted Thomas Tallis and William Byrd the monopoly on printing music and music paper in 1575. What was their first publication called?

6. Palestrina's *Missa Papae Marcelli* was dedicated to Pope Marcellus. How long did his papacy last?

7. What role did the composer Jacopo Peri take in the first production of his opera *Dafne* in 1598?

8. Where is the composer Orlando Gibbons buried?

9. During the reign of Louis XIV, which composer bought the right to be the only man in France to be allowed to put on operas, staging his first production on a converted tennis court?

10. Which Italian nobleman was responsible for Antonio Vivaldi's works being kept under lock and key, away from public performance, for around two centuries?

11. What was the name of the young soprano with whom the composer Antonio Vivaldi travelled around Europe for many years?

12. When Johann Sebastian Bach's parents died, he was sent to live with his older brother, an organist. What was his name?

13. In 1708, Johann Sebastian Bach was appointed organist to which nobleman?

14. Johann Sebastian Bach married his second wife in 1720. What was her name?

15. Johann Sebastian Bach and George Frideric Handel both suffered from cataracts. The same English surgeon botched operations to cure the problem on both men. What was his name?

16. Which of George Frideric Handel's operas gave him his first smash-hit success in London?

17. Domenico Scarlatti is best known for his piano compositions, but his father was a successful composer, too. What was his first name?

18. The Baroque composer Domenico Zipoli was born in Italy, but he emigrated to which continent to work as a Jesuit missionary?

19. The composer Carl Philipp Emanuel Bach worked for which king for some 28 years?

20. Carl Philipp Emanuel Bach was a famous keyboard player who wrote a much respected book on the subject. What was it called?

Round 40: The Year in Question

Each of these pairs (or trios) of musical and non-musical events took place in the same year in the 1900s. But what was the year in question? To help you, the answers are in chronological order.

1. William Walton is born in Oldham. — The United States purchases control of the Panama Canal.

2. The London Symphony Orchestra is founded. — The building of the Panama Canal begins.

3. Franz Lehár's operetta *The Merry Widow* has its first performance in Vienna. — Norway and Sweden become separate countries.

4. Maurice Ravel becomes Ralph Vaughan Williams's teacher in Paris for a three-month period. — Henry Ford produces his first Model T motor car.

5. In Gloucester, Ralph Vaughan Williams conducts the premiere of his *Fantasia on a Theme of Thomas Tallis* for string orchestra. — Dr Crippen becomes the first criminal suspect to be caught by radio when he is arrested on a ship off Canada.

6. Igor Stravinsky's ballet *Petrushka* has its first performance in Paris. — Amundsen arrives at the South Pole.

7. John Cage is born in Los Angeles. — The *Titanic* sinks.

8. Igor Stravinsky's ballet *The Rite of Spring* is given its first performance in Paris, causing something of an outrage. — D. H. Lawrence's *Sons and Lovers* is published.

9. Ralph Vaughan Williams's *London Symphony* has its first performance. — The First World War breaks out.

10. Sergei Rachmaninov packs his bags, gathers up his family and abandons his Russian homeland permanently. — The USA joins the First World War.

11. Leonard Bernstein is born in Massachusetts; Claude Debussy dies in Paris. — Peace breaks out, following the end of the First World War.

12. Edward Elgar's *Cello Concerto* is performed for the first time in London. — Man crosses the Atlantic for the first time in an aeroplane.

13. The Salzburg Festival opens its doors for the first time. — The first commercial radio broadcast takes place.

14. He hadn't wanted it to be played during his lifetime, so Camille Saint-Saëns's *Carnival of the Animals* finally receives its Paris premiere. — Insulin is discovered.

15. George Gershwin is the star soloist in the New York premiere of his *Rhapsody in Blue*. — Lenin dies.

16. Giacomo Puccini's opera *Turandot* receives its premiere in Milan under the baton of Arturo Toscanini. — The General Strike sweeps across Britain.

17. Sergei Rachmaninov might have been the soloist, but the premiere performance of his *Piano Concerto No. 4* in Philadelphia is far from being a crowd pleaser. — The first television transmission takes place.

18. Ralph Vaughan Williams's *Piano Concerto in C major* is given its first performance. — FM radio is invented.

19. Peter Maxwell Davies is born in Manchester. – The Joliot-Curies announce the creation of an artificial radioactive substance.

20. George Gershwin's opera *Porgy and Bess* is given its first performance in Boston. – T. S. Eliot's play *Murder in the Cathedral* has its first performance.

𝄢 **Round 41:** Fully Entitled

Can you identify each work's missing member of the nobility or military?

1. _____ *Ida*, opera by Gilbert and Sullivan

2. *The Tale of _____ Saltan*, opera by Nikolai Rimsky-Korsakov

3. ___ *Arthur*, semi-opera by Henry Purcell

4. *Oberto, ___ of Saint Boniface*, opera by Giuseppe Verdi

5. _____ *Bogey*, march by K. J. Alford

6. *The _____ of the Rose*, opera by Richard Strauss

7. *The _____ Waltz (Op. 437)* by Johann Strauss Jr

8. *The Grand _____* by Gilbert and Sullivan

9. ___ *Ory*, opera by Gioachino Rossini

10. *The Gypsy ___*, operetta by Johann Strauss Jr

11. ___ *for a Day*, opera by Giuseppe Verdi

12. ___ *Igor*, opera by Alexander Borodin

13. *A Life for the _____*, opera by Mikhail Glinka

14. *The _____ Concerto (Piano Concerto No. 5)* by Ludwig van Beethoven

15. *The ___ of Alba*, opera by Gaetano Donizetti

16. *The ___ of Luxembourg*, operetta by Franz Lehár

17. *The _____ String Quartet in C (Op. 76 No. 3)* by Franz Joseph Haydn

18. *The ___ in spite of Himself*, opera by Emmanuel Chabrier

19. *The _____ of the Pagodas*, ballet by Benjamin Britten

20. *Mitridate, ___ of Pontus*, opera by Wolfgang Amadeus Mozart

🎼 **Round 42:** Mind the Gap

Can you complete these titles by inserting the missing word? To help you along the way, all of the missing words are animals of one sort or another and each asterisk represents a missing letter.

1. Franz Schubert: ****** Quintet in A*

2. Frederick Delius: *On Hearing the First ****** in Spring*

3. Igor Stravinsky: *The Fire *****

4. Maurice Ravel: *Mother ***** Suite*

5. Ralph Vaughan Williams: *The **** Ascending*

6. Gioachino Rossini: *The Thieving *******

7. Camille Saint-Saëns: *The *****

8. Pyotr Ilyich Tchaikovsky: ***** Lake*

9. Jean Sibelius: *The **** of Tuonela*

10. Leoš Janáček: *The Cunning Little ******

11. Thomas Arne: *"Where the *** Sucks"*

12. Nikolai Rimsky-Korsakov: *The Flight of the **********

13. Giacomo Puccini: *Madame **********

14. Ralph Vaughan Williams: *The* *****

15. Sergei Prokofiev: *The Ugly* ********

16. Johann Sebastian Bach: "***** *May Safely Graze*"

17. Modest Mussorgsky: *The Song of the* ****

18. Sergei Prokofiev: *Peter and the* ****

19. Camille Saint-Saëns: *Carnival of the* *******

20. Francis Poulenc: *The Story of Babar, the Little* ********

🎧 **Round 43**: Odd One Out

Which is the odd one out — and why?

1. Mstislav Rostropovich, Evgeny Kissin, Julian Lloyd-
   Webber, Steven Isserlis, Yo Yo Ma

2. Glockenspiel, Marimba, Castanets, Cornet, Triangle,
   Timpani

3. Natalie Clein, Maxim Vengerov, Nicola Benedetti,
   Joshua Bell, Daniel Hope, Nigel Kennedy

4. Carl Philipp Emanuel Bach, Johann Christian Bach,
   Johann Sebastian Bach, Johann Christoph Bach,
   Wilhelm Friedemann Bach

5. *Sylvia, The Rite of Spring, Swan Lake, Daphnis and
   Chloé, Petrushka, Carmen*

6. *La Bohème, Carmen, Tosca, Madame Butterfly, Turandot,
   Gianni Schicchi*

7. *Veritable Flabby Preludes (for a Dog), Sketches and
   Exasperations of a Big Boob Made of Wood, Five Grins
   or Mona Lisa's Moustache, Waltz of the Chocolate
   Almonds, Étude on Consideration of a Striped Ocelot,
   Things Seen from the Right and Left without Spectacles*

8. *Parsifal, Das Rheingold, Die Walküre, Siegfried,
   Götterdämmerung*

9. *Star Wars, Rain Man, Raiders of the Lost Ark, Superman,
   E.T., Harry Potter 1, 2 and 3*

10. Domenico Scarlatti, Johann Sebastian Bach, George Frideric Handel, Domenico Zipoli

11. *The Marriage of Figaro, Turandot, Don Giovanni, Così fan tutte, The Magic Flute*

12. *The Barber of Seville, The Thieving Magpie, William Tell, Otello*

13. George Gershwin, Felix Mendelssohn, Henry Purcell, Camille Saint-Saëns

14. Gustav Mahler, Gaetano Donizetti, Robert Schumann, Bedřich Smetana

15. Alexander Borodin, Mily Balakirev, Nikolai Rimsky-Korsakov, Pyotr Ilyich Tchaikovsky, César Cui, Modest Mussorgsky

16. Domenico Zipoli, Antonín Dvořák, Bedřich Smetana, Josef Suk, Leoš Janáček

17. Pablo Martín de Sarasate, Enrique Granados, Manuel de Falla, Isaac Albéniz, Heitor Villa-Lobos

18. *Trial by Jury, The Thieving Magpie, The Pirates of Penzance, HMS Pinafore, The Yeoman of the Guard*

19. Arnold Bax, Hubert Parry, Samuel Coleridge-Taylor, George Butterworth, George Gershwin

20. Emmanuel Chabrier, Charles-Marie Widor, Max Bruch, Joseph Canteloube, Jules Massenet

🎵 **Round 44:** Quick Fire (Fiendish)

1. Wolfgang Amadeus Mozart originally fell in love with his eventual wife's sister. What was her name?

2. Who wrote the 1831 play *Mozart and Salieri*?

3. How many years after Wolfgang Amadeus Mozart was Ludwig van Beethoven born?

4. How old was Ludwig van Beethoven when he died?

5. The composer Louis Spohr was widely respected as a teacher in his day. He wrote a book on the subject that he taught. What was it called?

6. When he was a boy, the German composer Carl Maria von Weber used to travel the country with his father's company. What sort of company was it?

7. At what age did Gioachino Rossini suddenly stop writing opera altogether, despite penning operatic hit after operatic hit?

8. In 1815, how many songs did Franz Schubert compose?

9. Franz Schubert only ever gave one major concert, in the year of his death, but this event was overshadowed by the arrival of which other famous composer in Vienna at the same time?

10. What job did Hector Berlioz's father do?

11. In what year did the actress Harriet Smithson finally give in and marry Hector Berlioz?

12. Which 20th-century French composer wrote *L'horloge de flore*?

13. How do Americans refer to what we Brits call "crotchets" in musical notation?

14. How many sexual conquests did the servant Leporello claim for his master Don Giovanni in the "*Catalogue Aria*" in Mozart's opera *Don Giovanni*?

15. The great tenor Enrico Caruso died at the age of 48. In how many different operas did he sing the leading tenor role at the Metropolitan Opera House in New York during his lifetime?

16. How old was Georges Bizet when he wrote his first symphony?

17. What was the name of Mikhail Glinka's first opera?

18. Modest Mussorgsky didn't actually orchestrate much of his opera *Boris Godunov* or his big hit *Night on a Bare Mountain*. Who did it for him?

19. What was the name of the rich widow who funded Pyotr Ilyich Tchaikovsky's work on the condition that they should never meet?

20. *Vltava* is the most popular section of Bedřich Smetana's *Má Vlast*. How many other sections are there?

🔳 **Round 45:** Enigmas

Solve the cryptic crossword-style clues to identify each of these composers.

1. Composer who made his start in Italy? (7)

2. Z-list composer? (5)

3. Composer's initial nag about Rachmaninov's first, in other words. (5)

4. Our Queen's up and down about George, the first's, composer. (5)

5. Composer cogitates: Latin was removed. (7)

6. Composer in grip of showbiz ethos. (5)

7. Orchestra (US) serenades secret composer. (7)

8. There's a bend – between a long, long way to run and a drop of golden sun! (5)

9. Composer met Verdi on way out. (10)

10. Composer's connection found in Gregorio Allegri, initially (6)

🎵 **Round 46:** Mix & Match

Match these composers to their musical eras.

You can choose from:
Early, Baroque, Classical, Romantic, Modern.

1. Johann Sebastian Bach

2. Leonard Bernstein

3. Georges Bizet

4. Benjamin Britten

5. Anton Bruckner

6. John Cage

7. Léo Delibes

8. Karl Ditters von Dittersdorf

9. Guillaume Dufay

10. John Dunstable

11. Gustav Mahler

12. Johann Pachelbel

13. Niccolò Paganini

14. John Rutter

15. Robert Schumann

16. Arthur Sullivan

17. Thomas Tallis

18. John Tavener

19. Antonio Vivaldi

20. Carl Maria von Weber

Round 47: Order! Order!

Put these composers in the order of their birth:

1. César Franck

2. Claudio Monteverdi

3. Dmitri Shostakovich

4. Edvard Grieg

5. Edward Elgar

6. Felix Mendelssohn

7. Franz Joseph Haydn

8. George Gershwin

9. Henry Purcell

10. Hildegard of Bingen

11. Igor Stravinsky

12. Johann Sebastian Bach

13. Johann Strauss Sr

14. Jules Massenet

15. Ludwig van Beethoven

16. Max Bruch

17. Patrick Hawes

18. Philip Glass

19. Samuel Barber

20. Wolfgang Amadeus Mozart

Round 48: Quick Fire (Fiendish)

1. What big job in New York did Antonín Dvořák hold in the 1890s?

2. How many years separate the birthdays of Johann Strauss Sr and Johann Strauss Jr?

3. To what philanthropic enterprise did Giuseppe Verdi bequeath his considerable riches?

4. How many years after Johannes Brahms was Max Bruch born?

5. Which other famous French composer took over from Camille Saint-Saëns as organist at the church of La Madeleine in Paris?

6. In what sort of office did Edward Elgar work as a young man, before turning to music full-time?

7. In Edward Elgar's *Enigma Variations*, what was the name of the person on whom *Nimrod* was based?

8. After which animal was the French composer Gabriel Fauré nicknamed by his friends?

9. In 1897, Gustav Mahler became the conductor of which great opera company?

10. What was the name of Sergei Rachmaninov's first opera, which he wrote when he was just 19 years old?

11. What mark did Pyotr Ilyich Tchaikovsky give to Sergei Rachmaninov when the latter played for him at the Moscow Conservatory?

12. What was the name of the hypnotist to whom Sergei Rachmaninov dedicated his *Piano Concerto No. 2*?

13. Which was Gustav Holst's main instrument as a player?

14. While Frederick Delius was living in America, he took lessons from which American organist?

15. What was the name of Frederick Delius's amanuensis?

16. Which 20th-century composer is credited with inventing "serialism"?

17. For which orchestra did Béla Bartók compose his *Concerto for Orchestra*?

18. Aaron Copland changed his surname. What was it originally?

19. In 1934, Stalin stormed out of a performance of an opera by Dmitri Shostakovich, which resulted in the composer being branded an "enemy of the people". What was the name of the opera?

20. Benjamin Britten was born in which Suffolk town?

Round 49: Mix & Match

Match the list of first names to the surname of each of the composers.

You can choose from:
Albéniz, Allegri, Berlioz, Brahms, Delius, Gibbons, Glinka, Górecki, Liszt, McCartney, Mussorgsky, Offenbach, Peri, Ravel, Rimsky-Korsakov, Salieri, Schoenberg, Smetana, Spohr, Vaughan Williams.

1. Antonio

2. Arnold

3. Bedřich

4. Franz

5. Frederick

6. Gregorio

7. Hector

8. Henryk

9. Isaac

10. Jacopo

11. Jacques

12. Johannes

13. Louis

14. Maurice

15. Mikhail

16. Modest

17. Nikolai

18. Orlando

19. Paul

20. Ralph

🎵 **Round 50:** On the Street Where You Live

Name these classical music types – some of whom were famous visitors to our shores, while others were equally well-known natives.

1. Who stayed at Abbey Street in Dublin in 1742 for the premiere of his best-known oratorio?

2. Which composer was born at the Old Vicarage, Down Ampney Road, Down Ampney, on 12 October 1872?

3. Who stayed at King's Lodge, Cambridge, in 1894 on a visit to receive his honorary degree? Once he'd received his honour, he went to the local post office and sent a telegram home to Bergen, signed "Dr".

4. Which legendary choral conductor and organist, famous not least for his volumes of Carols for Choirs, was born in Newquay on 30 December 1919?

5. Who stayed in Worcester in 1884 while conducting his *Stabat Mater* and *Symphony No. 6* at the Shire Hall – with a young Elgar in the first violin section?

6. Which composer's family home was Cefn Bryntalch, in Abermule?

7. Who stayed at the Lion Hotel in Leeds while performing with his orchestra at the Music Hall in 1838? He wouldn't have played his famous *Radetzky March*, though – it hadn't been written yet.

8. Who was eventually buried in St Peter's Cemetery, in Limpsfield, Surrey, in 1935, with Vaughan Williams and Thomas Beecham among those attending the service?

9. Which Polish pianist was described as "… spare in frame" with "… an almost painful air of feebleness" following his concert at Crumpsall in 1848?

10. Which military-sounding conductor was born on 29 April 1895 at Bath Villas, in Ashford, Kent?

11. Which towering Russian played his *Second Piano Concerto* at the Free Trade Hall, Manchester, on 29 January 1914?

12. Which future Master of the King's Music spent his honeymoon in 1889 on the Isle of Wight, at Shanklin and Ventnor?

13. Which Italian opera composer stayed at the Adelphi Hotel, Liverpool, in 1911, while supervising a performance of his *La fanciulla del West*?

14. Which great conductor and founder of the London Philharmonic Orchestra was born in Arthur Street, St Helens, on 29 April 1879?

15. Which diabolical Italian violinist stayed at Simpson's Hotel, Edinburgh, during a series of concerts in 1833? (And we are using diabolical in its original sense here – he was a fantastic player by all accounts.)

16. Name the 'amanuensis' born on 22 April 1906, in Scarborough?

17. Which German composer stayed in Glasgow in 1829 while on a famous Scottish tour that produced, amongst other things, a musical picture of Fingal's Cave?

18. Which conductor and champion of Elgar was born at 6 Abbot's Road, Chester, on 8 April 1889?

19. Which French musical pioneer stayed at the Grand Hotel, Eastbourne, in 1905, looking out to sea and putting the finishing touches to his La Mer?

20. Which organist and composer, the "forgotten master of the North" commemorated in a Browning poem, was born in Newcastle-upon-Tyne in 1709?

🎵 **Round 51:** Whose Aria Is It Anyway?

From which opera is each aria or chorus taken?

1. *"Che gelida manina"*

2. *"Brindisi"*

3. *"Anvil Chorus"*

4. *"Lensky's Aria"*

5. *"Va pensiero"*

6. *"Where'er you walk"*

7. *"Mon coeur s'ouvre à ta voix"*

8. *"La donna è mobile"*

9. *"Summertime"*

10. *"E lucevan le stelle"*

11. *"Champagne Aria"*

12. *"Una furtiva lagrima"*

13. *"Che farò senza Euridice"*

14. *"Der Vogelfänger bin ich ja"*

15. *"Chi il bel sogno di Doretta"*

16. *"Bella figlia dell'amore"*

17. *"Dove sono i bei momenti"*

18. *"The Catalogue Aria"*

19. *"Habanera"*

20. *"Humming Chorus"*

Round 52: Cinematic Sounds

Match the classical work to the film in which it featured.

You can choose from:
2001: A Space Odyssey, Apocalypse Now, Babe,
A Beautiful Mind, Bend It Like Beckham, Billy Elliot,
Brassed Off, Bridget Jones's Diary, A Clockwork Orange,
The Ladykillers, Natural Born Killers, Out of Africa,
Platoon, Pretty Woman, A Room with a View, The
Shawshank Redemption, Shine, The Silence of the Lambs,
Trainspotting, What's Opera, Doc?

1. Johann Sebastian Bach: *Goldberg Variations*

2. Samuel Barber: *Adagio for Strings*

3. Ludwig van Beethoven: *Symphony No. 9*

4. Georges Bizet: *Habanera* from *Carmen*

5. Luigi Boccherini: *Minuet*

6. George Frideric Handel: "*Hallelujah Chorus*" from *Messiah*

7. Wolfgang Amadeus Mozart: *Clarinet Concerto*

8. Wolfgang Amadeus Mozart: "*Che soave zeffiretto*" from *The Marriage of Figaro*

9. Wolfgang Amadeus Mozart: *Piano Sonata No. 11*

10. Carl Orff: *Carmina Burana*

11. Giacomo Puccini: *"Chi il bel sogno di Doretta"* from *La rondine*

12. Giacomo Puccini: *"Nessun dorma"* from *Turandot*

13. Sergei Rachmaninov: *Piano Concerto No. 3*

14. Joaquín Rodrigo: Concierto de Aranjuez

15. Camille Saint-Saëns: *Organ Symphony No. 3*

16. Richard Strauss: *Also sprach Zarathustra*

17. Pyotr Ilyich Tchaikovsky: *Swan Lake*

18. Antonio Vivaldi: *The Four Seasons*

19. Richard Wagner: *Tannhäuser*

20. Richard Wagner: *Ride of the Valkyries*

🎵 **Round 53:** Operatic Dons

1. In which opera by Gaetano Donizetti did Don Alfonso appear?

2. In which opera by Wolfgang Amadeus Mozart did Don Alfonso appear?

3. In which operetta by W. S. Gilbert and Arthur Sullivan did Don Alhambra del Bolero appear?

4. In which opera by Gioachino Rossini did Don Alonso appear?

5. In which opera by Jean-Philippe Rameau did Don Alvar appear?

6. In which opera by Giuseppe Verdi did Don Álvaro appear?

7. In which opera by Wolfgang Amadeus Mozart did Don Basilio appear?

8. In which opera by Gioachino Rossini did Don Basilio appear?

9. In which opera by Jean-Philippe Rameau did Don Carlos appear?

10. In which opera by Wolfgang Amadeus Mozart did Don Cassandro appear?

11. In which opera by Wolfgang Amadeus Mozart did Don Curzio appear?

12. In which opera by Ludwig van Beethoven did Don Fernando appear?

13. In which opera by Wolfgang Amadeus Mozart did Don Giovanni appear?

14. In which opera by Georges Bizet did Don José appear?

15. In which opera by Frederick Delius did Don José Martinez appear?

16. In which opera by Wolfgang Amadeus Mozart did Don Ottavio appear?

17. In which opera by Ludwig van Beethoven did Don Pizarro appear?

18. In which opera by Wolfgang Amadeus Mozart did Don Polidoro appear?

19. In which opera by Henry Purcell did Don Quixote appear?

20. Don Carlo appeared in three operas by Giuseppe Verdi. Can you name one of them?

♭♭ **Round 54:** Mix & Match

Match the following famous Christmas works and carol tunes to their composers.

You can choose from:
Benjamin Britten, Victor Hely-Hutchinson, Gustav Holst, Felix Mendelssohn, Ralph Vaughan Williams.

1. *"Hark the Herald Angels Sing"*

2. *"See Amid the Winter's Snow"*

3. *Ceremony of Carols*

4. *Fantasia on Christmas Carols*

5. *A Carol Symphony*

Match the dates to each of the classical music eras.

You can choose from:
Baroque, Classical, Early, Modern, Romantic.

1. Before 1600

2. 1600–1750

3. 1750–1830

4. 1830–1900

5. 1900–today

The Planets Suite is Gustav Holst's best-known work. Can you match the planets with their astrological influences?

You can choose from:
Jollity, Magic, Old Age, Mysticism, Peace, War.

1. Mars

2. Venus

3. Jupiter

4. Uranus

5. Saturn

6. Neptune

🔘 **Round 55:** The Year in Question

Each of these pairs (or trios) of musical and non-musical events took place in the same year in the 1900s. But what was the year in question? To help you, the answers are in chronological order.

1. Sergei Prokofiev's *Peter and the Wolf* is given its premiere in Moscow. — The Spanish Civil War breaks out.

2. Samuel Barber's *Adagio for Strings* is performed for the first time in New York. — The uranium atom is split for the first time.

3. Aaron Copland's ballet *Rodeo* is given its first performance in New York. — The Battle of El Alamein takes place.

4. The Edinburgh International Festival opens. — India becomes independent.

5. Benjamin Britten's Aldeburgh Festival opens. — The state of Israel is founded.

6. Ralph Vaughan Williams's *Sinfonia Antartica* is given its debut in Manchester. — Mount Everest is conquered for the first time.

7. Ralph Vaughan Williams dies. — Krushchev becomes leader of the Soviet Union and de Gaulle becomes leader of France.

8. Benjamin Britten's *War Requiem* is performed for the first time, in the newly rebuilt Coventry Cathedral. — Marilyn Monroe is found dead.

9. Igor Stravinsky dies in New York. — War breaks out between India and Pakistan.

10. Peter Maxwell Davies's opera *Taverner* is given its premiere at the Royal Opera House in London's Covent Garden. — Britain imposes direct rule on Northern Ireland.

11. Dmitri Shostakovich dies in Moscow. — The Vietnam War ends.

12. Philip Glass composes his opera *Einstein on the Beach*. — Mao Zedong dies.

13. The film *Out of Africa*, with score by John Barry, is released. — Mikhail Gorbachev becomes leader of the Soviet Union.

14. John Adams finishes his opera *Nixon in China*. — The *Herald of Free Enterprise* capsizes off Zeebrugge.

15. The towering Austrian conductor Herbert von Karajan dies. — The Tiananmen Square massacre takes place in China.

16. The first Three Tenors Concert takes place on the eve of the World Cup Final in Rome. — Iraq invades Kuwait.

17. Classic FM begins broadcasting classical music across the UK. — Bill Clinton becomes President of the USA.

18. The Henry Wood Promenade Concerts celebrate their 100th season. — The Channel Tunnel opens.

19. One of the greatest opera houses anywhere in the world, Teatro La Fenice in Venice, is ravaged by fire. — The former French President, François Mitterrand, dies.

20. The violinist and conductor Yehudi Menuhin dies. — The Euro is launched across most of Europe, but not in the UK.

Round 56: Enigmas

Solve our final selection of cryptic clues to reveal ten well-known classical works.

1. Beethoven's extra job was playing piano? (9,6)

2. The redhead scores with Frankie's band in the hotel, with a pizza. (3,4,7)

3. If winter is, I hear, on the left, then where's summer? (3,4,2,6)

4. Music for a short German cavalier? (4,6,10)

5. Mechanics who don't need a mic? (6)

6. Best man remembers this and the bike? (3,4,5)

7. Cuba ran airman out for old, spicy work. (7,6)

8. 42.56759330758526 squared? (4,8)

9. Colour from Breg sky to Black Sea. (4,6)

10. Off peg entry for rock legend? (4,4)

Round 57: Order! Order!

Put these musical note values in the correct order, starting with the note that lasts for the longest number of beats:

1. Breve

2. Crotchet

3. Demisemiquaver

4. Hemidemisemiquaver

5. Minim

6. Quaver

7. Semibreve

8. Semiquaver

Put the operas that make up Wagner's *Ring Cycle* in their correct order of performance:

1. *Das Rheingold*

2. *Die Walküre*

3. *Götterdämmerung*

4. *Siegfried*

The composer Igor Stravinsky liked to move around. Put the following countries in the order in which he lived in them:

1. France

2. Russia

3. Switzerland

4. USA

Put the following ballets in the order in which they were written:

1. Adolphe Adam: *Giselle*

2. Léo Delibes: *Coppélia*

3. Igor Stravinsky: *Pulcinella*

4. Pyotr Ilyich Tchaikovsky: *The Sleeping Beauty*

◉ **Round 58:** Name that Composer

Each of the groups of works listed below was written by one person. Can you name that composer?

1. *Gloria, The Story of Babar, the Little Elephant, Organ Concerto*

2. *Rhapsody in Blue, Porgy and Bess, An American in Paris*

3. *Fanfare for the Common Man, Rodeo, Appalachian Spring*

4. *Spitfire Prelude and Fugue, Crown Imperial, Orb and Sceptre*

5. *Jazz Suites, The Assault on Beautiful Gorky, The Gadfly*

6. *The Young Person's Guide to the Orchestra, Peter Grimes, Ceremony of Carols*

7. *Candide, Chichester Psalms, West Side Story*

8. *Spiegel im Spiegel, Cantus in Memoriam Benjamin Britten, Tabula Rasa*

9. *The Protecting Veil, The Lamb, Song for Athene*

10. *Koyaanisqatsi, The Hours, Kundun*

11. *A Gaelic Blessing, For the Beauty of the Earth, The Candlelight Carol*

12. *Adiemus: Songs of Sanctuary, Palladio, The Armed Man: A Mass for Peace*

13. *Liverpool Oratorio, Standing Stone, "Ecce Cor Meum"*

14. *Le Onde, Eden Roc, I Giorni*

15. *The Dying Swan, The Hitchhiker's Guide to the Galaxy, Once Around the Sun*

16. *Star Wars, Harry Potter 1, 2 and 3, Schindler's List*

17. *Out of Africa, Dances with Wolves, The Beyondness of Things*

18. *Gangs of New York, The Silence of the Lambs, The Lord of the Rings*

19. *Braveheart, Titanic, A Beautiful Mind*

20. *Gladiator, Mission: Impossible II, My Beautiful Laundrette*

𝄢 **Round 59:** Heavenly Music

Match each of the composers to their star sign.

You can choose from:
Aquarius, Pisces, Aries, Taurus, Gemini, Cancer, Leo, Virgo, Libra, Scorpio, Sagittarius, Capricorn.

1. Ludwig van Beethoven

2. Hector Berlioz

3. Johannes Brahms

4. Max Bruch

5. Aaron Copland

6. Claude Debussy

7. Frederick Delius

8. Léo Delibes

9. Edward Elgar

10. George Gershwin

11. Alexander Glazunov

12. Christoph Willibald Gluck

13. Edvard Grieg

14. George Frideric Handel

15. Franz Joseph Haydn

16. Gustav Holst

17. Gustav Mahler

18. Wolfgang Amadeus Mozart

19. Johann Pachelbel

20. Giacomo Puccini

21. Johann Strauss Jr

22. Sergei Rachmaninov

23. Dmitri Shostakovich

24. Pyotr Ilyich Tchaikovsky

🎵 **Round 60:** Anything Goes

Before we finish, here's a final set of twenty questions to test your musical grey matter:

1. What is the name of the chamber orchestra that is resident in the Sage Gateshead?

2. Which is the odd one out in this list? Deutsche Grammophon; Decca; RCA Victor; Mercury Classics

3. What is the name of the Hong Kong-based entrepreneur who launched the Naxos record label?

4. Two Classic FM presenters have appeared on the television show *Top of the Pops*. One is the Blur bass player, Alex James. But can you name the other?

5. Name the composer who sprang to international attention after his motet *Ubi Caritas* was performed at the marriage of the Duke and Duchess of Cambridge.

6. Who is the choirmaster who, along with the composer from the preceding question, had the Christmas number one in the pop charts alongside the Military Wives choir?

7. Which film-music composer was given the Lifetime Achievement award at the 2012 Classic BRITs, to mark his 80th birthday?

8. Which Dutch violin superstar made a cameo appearance as himself on 'Ramsay Street' in the long-running Australian soap opera *Neighbours*?

9. The French composer Claude Debussy's mother was a seamstress, but what did his father's shop sell?

10. Which member of the Bee Gees composed a classical work *The Titanic Requiem*, which received its premiere shortly before his death in 2012?

11. The tenor Andrea Bocelli trained in what profession, before giving it up to concentrate on his singing?

12. Which soprano's first three albums were entitled *Premiere*, *Second Nature* and *Living A Dream*?

13. The band B. Bumble and the Stingers had a UK chart number one with *Nut Rocker* in 1962. This was based on music from which ballet?

14. True or false … Edward Elgar invented the "Elgar Sulphuretted Hydrogen Apparatus" – a device for synthesizing hydrogen sulphide.

15. In October 2010, the tenor Alfie Boe took on the role of Jean Valjean in a concert performance of which musical at the O2 Arena in London to celebrate the show's 25th anniversary?

16. Two great composers wrote music dedicated to Athalia. Handel was one. Who was the other?

17. Which composer is thought to be among the first to cut a record of his own music – a *Hungarian Dance* recorded in 1889 by an associate of Thomas Edison?

18. Classic FM shares its 7 September birthday with the poet Edith Sitwell. Which composer collaborated with Sitwell in 1922 in their "entertainment" *Façade*?

19. In 1952, John Cage famously wrote his silent work, *4'33"*, in which the performer is instructed not to play the music written. Into how many movements is the work divided?

20. Which floral piece of music was adapted by, among others, Beethoven, Mendelssohn and Flotow, having been originally an Irish air called *Castle Hyde*?

THE ANSWERS

You will find all of the answers to the 1,150 questions asked over the past 130 or so pages in this next section of our book. Keep your score for each of the 60 rounds as you work your way through the book, and then add them all up to give yourself a grand total score out of 1,150 at the end.

🎵 **Round 1:** Quick Fire (Easier)

Score /20

1. Play with a spikier sound, detaching the notes from each other
2. Works
3. Goretski
4. Overture
5. Luciano Pavarotti, Plácido Domingo and José Carreras
6. James Galway
7. Quiet Loud
8. Tuba
9. Stephen Sondheim
10. Aldeburgh
11. Peter Maxwell Davies
12. Adam Smith
13. Russia over France
14. 104
15. Soft Machine
16. Brother and sister
17. *Piano Concerto No. 2.* They were published in the wrong order.
18. *Boléro*
19. Foie gras and truffles
20. Cambridge

● **Round 2:** Cinematic Sounds

Score /20

1. *Dangerous Moonlight*
2. *Dances with Wolves*
3. *The Magnificent Seven*
4. *The Snowman*
5. *The Heiress*
6. *Pride and Prejudice*
7. *Sense and Sensibility*
8. *The Hours*
9. *Alien*
10. *Titanic*
11. *Robin Hood, Prince of Thieves*
12. *The Mission*
13. *The Piano*
14. *Lieutenant Kijé*
15. *The Gadfly*
16. *The Lord of the Rings*
17. *49th Parallel*
18. *Henry V*
19. *Superman*
20. *Gladiator*

● **Round 3:** Quick Fire (Easier)

Score /20

1. *Symphony No. 8*
2. She was a famous concert pianist and she composed as well.

3. Johann Strauss Sr

4. Johann Strauss Jr

5. The Divine Comedy

6. The Red Priest

7. John Taverner was born first.

8. Pope Gregory I

9. Hildegard of Bingen

10. Rebirth

11. Karl Jenkins

12. Thomas Cromwell

13. Work

14. The Vatican

15. He speared his foot with his conducting baton, dying of gangrene two months later.

16. *Te Deum*

17. Concerto Grosso

18. They are all *Canons*.

19. *"When I am laid in earth"*

20. EMI Classics

🎵 **Round 4:** Musical Colours

Score /20

1. Green

2. Blue

3. Gold

4. Red

5. Purple

6. Green
7. Blue
8. Silver
9. Yellow
10. Colour (this is the odd one out we warned you about)
11. Gold and silver
12. Orange
13. Golden
14. Blue
15. White
16. Silver
17. Black
18. Blue
19. Red
20. Blue

🔘 **Round 5:** The Year in Question

Score /20

1. 1703
2. 1711
3. 1717
4. 1720
5. 1724
6. 1727
7. 1727
8. 1736

9. 1739
10. 1740
11. 1742
12. 1752
13. 1756
14. 1759
15. 1770
16. 1782
17. 1786
18. 1794
19. 1797
20. 1799

🔳 **Round 6:** Order! Order!

Score /20

1. Catherina Dorothea (1708)
2. Wilhelm Friedemann (1710)
3. Maria Sophia (1713)
4. Johann Christoph (1713)
5. Carl Philipp Emanuel (1714)
6. Johann Gottfried Bernhard (1715)
7. Leopold August (1718)
8. Christiana Sophia Henrietta (1723)
9. Gottfried Heinrich (1724)
10. Christian Gottlieb (1725)
11. Elisabeth Juliana Friederike (1726)
12. Ernst Andreas (1727)

13. Regina Johanna (1728)
14. Christiana Benedicta (1730)
15. Christiana Dorothea (1731)
16. Johann Christoph Friedrich (1732)
17. Johann August Abraham (1733)
18. Johann Christian (1735)
19. Johanna Carolina (1737)
20. Regina Susanna (1742)

🎵 **Round 7:** Quick Fire (Easier)

Score /20

1. St John and St Matthew
2. He added up the alphabetical position of each of the component letters of his surname.
3. In the attic of their home
4. King George I
5. Westminster Abbey
6. Dittersdorf
7. Prince Archbishop of Salzburg
8. Antonio Salieri
9. Vienna
10. Lesley Garrett
11. Ralph Vaughan Williams
12. Holland
13. *Fidelio*
14. Romantic
15. Navy

16. *The Arabian Nights*
17. Czech
18. A carpet
19. Liverpool
20. Worcestershire

// **Round 8:** True or False

Score /20

1. True
2. True
3. True
4. True
5. True
6. True
7. True
8. False — a piccolo is smaller than a flute.
9. False — a sackbut is an early version of a trombone.
10. False — he retired 60 years earlier, in 1913.
11. True
12. False — he is a pianist.
13. False — he did visit Scotland.
14. False — he's famous for his works for piano.
15. True
16. True
17. True
18. True

19. True

20. False — he lived to the age of 70, having earned considerable riches along the way.

🎵 **Round 9:** Quick Fire (Easier)

Score /20

1. *Enigma Variations*
2. "*None shall sleep*"
3. Sting
4. He picked her name out of a hat.
5. Ralph was pronounced "Rafe" to rhyme with "safe". Any word that rhymes with this is correct.
6. Sergei Rachmaninov's *Piano Concerto No. 2*
7. St Paul's School for Girls.
8. Bradford
9. There was a near-riot among members of the audience.
10. Stalin
11. Rhône-Poulenc
12. *Porgy and Bess*
13. Georg Solti
14. Yuri Gagarin
15. *4'33"*
16. Ringo Starr
17. Liverpool Cathedral
18. "*Ecce Cor Meum*"
19. *Pure*
20. Car mechanic

🎼 **Round 10:** Birthday Bonanza

Score /20

1. Marc-Antoine Charpentier
2. Georg Philipp Telemann
3. George Frideric Handel
4. Carl Philipp Emanuel Bach
5. Johann Christian Bach
6. Karl Ditters von Dittersdorf
7. Gioachino Rossini
8. Mikhail Glinka
9. Richard Wagner
10. Johann Strauss Jr
11. Alexander Borodin
12. Camille Saint-Saëns
13. Georges Bizet
14. Sergei Rachmaninov
15. Béla Bartók
16. Joaquín Rodrigo
17. John Barry
18. Karl Jenkins
19. Howard Shore
20. Joby Talbot

🎹 **Round 11:** Enigmas

Score /10

1. De Falla
2. Field

3. Vaughan Williams
4. Sibelius
5. Shostakovich
6. Paganini
7. Purcell
8. Saint-Saëns
9. Stravinsky
10. Chopin

♪ **Round 12:** They Said What?

Score /20

1. Johann Sebastian Bach
2. Arnold Bax
3. Ludwig van Beethoven
4. Hector Berlioz
5. Leonard Bernstein
6. Johannes Brahms
7. Benjamin Britten
8. Aaron Copland
9. Gustav Holst
10. Pietro Mascagni
11. Wolfgang Amadeus Mozart
12. Niccolò Paganini
13. Sergei Rachmaninov
14. Maurice Ravel
15. Gioachino Rossini
16. Robert Schumann

17. Jean Sibelius
18. Richard Strauss
19. Igor Stravinsky
20. Pyotr Ilyich Tchaikovsky

♭♭ **Round 13:** Mix & Match

Score /20

1. The Philosopher
2. Lamentation
3. Mercury
4. Farewell
5. Maria Theresa
6. The Passion
7. The Schoolmaster
8. Fire
9. The Distracted
10. The Hunt
11. The Bear
12. The Hen
13. The Queen
14. Oxford
15. Surprise
16. Miracle
17. Military
18. Clock
19. Drum Roll
20. London

Round 14: Order! Order!

Score /22

Musical Speeds:
1. Largo
2. Adagio
3. Andante
4. Allegretto
5. Allegro
6. Presto

Voices:
1. Soprano
2. Mezzo-soprano
3. Tenor
4. Baritone
5. Bass-baritone
6. Bass

Masters of the King's/Queen's Music:
1. Nicholas Lanier (1625)
2. William Boyce (1755)
3. Edward Elgar (1924)
4. Arnold Bax (1942)
5. Arthur Bliss (1953)
6. Peter Maxwell Davies (2004)

Mozart's Names
1. Johannes
2. Chrysostomus
3. Wolfgangus
4. Amadeus

🎵 **Round 15:** Mix & Match

Score /20

1. London
2. Liverpool
3. Amsterdam
4. New York
5. Los Angeles
6. Edinburgh
7. Gateshead
8. Poole
9. Cardiff
10. Manchester
11. Birmingham
12. Vienna
13. Basingstoke
14. Belfast
15. Snape
16. Leipzig
17. Zurich
18. Croydon
19. Washington
20. Glasgow

🔊 **Round 16:** The Year in Question

Score /20

1. 1800
2. 1811

3. 1813
4. 1814
5. 1815
6. 1819
7. 1823
8. 1833
9. 1836
10. 1838
11. 1840
12. 1842
13. 1844
14. 1845
15. 1846
16. 1847
17. 1848
18. 1849
19. 1853
20. 1854

🎵 **Round 17:** Famous Last Words

Score /20

1. Gustav Mahler
2. Ludwig van Beethoven
3. Alban Berg
4. Modest Mussorgsky
5. Gustav Holst
6. Hector Berlioz

7. Georges Bizet
8. Ferruccio Busoni
9. Enrico Caruso
10. Albert, Prince Consort
11. Frédéric Chopin
12. Kathleen Ferrier
13. Edvard Greig
14. Franz Lehár
15. Alexander Borodin
16. Jean-Baptiste Lully
17. Felix Mendelssohn
18. Saint Cecilia
19. Frederick the Great
20. Wolfgang Amadeus Mozart

🎼 **Round 18:** Whose Aria Is It Anyway?

Score /20
1. Giuseppe Verdi: *Aida*
2. Gioachino Rossini: *The Barber of Seville*
3. Giacomo Puccini: *La Bohème*
4. Georges Bizet: *Carmen*
5. Léo Delibes: *Lakmé*
6. Wolfgang Amadeus Mozart: *The Marriage of Figaro*
7. Giuseppe Verdi: *Nabucco*
8. Georges Bizet: *The Pearl Fishers*
9. Henry Purcell: *Dido and Aeneas*
10. Giuseppe Verdi: *La traviata*

11. Giuseppe Verdi: *Otello*
12. Antonín Dvořák: *Rusalka*
13. Vincenzo Bellini: *Norma*
14. Giacomo Puccini: *Turandot*
15. Wolfgang Amadeus Mozart: *Don Giovanni*
16. Ludwig van Beethoven: *Fidelio*
17. Giacomo Puccini: *Gianni Schicchi*
18. Pietro Mascagni: *Cavalleria rusticana*
19. Giacomo Puccini: *Tosca*
20. George Gershwin: *Porgy and Bess*

🎵 **Round 19:** Definitive Mix & Match

Score /20

1. Trio
2. Oratorio
3. A capella
4. Quintet
5. Allegro
6. Toccata
7. Aria
8. Chamber music
9. Concerto
10. Gavotte
11. Legato
12. Libretto
13. Kapellmeister
14. Quartet

15. Movement
16. Intermezzo
17. Adagio
18. Opus
19. Cadenza
20. Lied

🎼 **Round 20:** Name That Composer

Score /20

1. Henry Purcell
2. Antonio Vivaldi
3. Johann Sebastian Bach
4. George Frideric Handel
5. Franz Joseph Haydn
6. Wolfgang Amadeus Mozart
7. Ludwig van Beethoven
8. Franz Schubert
9. Hector Berlioz
10. Felix Mendelssohn
11. Frédéric Chopin
12. Robert Schumann
13. Franz Liszt
14. Georges Bizet
15. Mikhail Glinka
16. Alexander Borodin
17. Modest Mussorgsky
18. Nikolai Rimsky-Korsakov

19. Pyotr Ilyich Tchaikovsky

20. Antonín Dvořák

🎵 **Round 21:** Quick Fire (Intermediate)

Score /20

1. Elephant
2. Francis Poulenc
3. Henrik Ibsen
4. John Field
5. English horn
6. London Symphony Orchestra
7. Catrin Finch
8. Adolphe Sax
9. Dietrich Buxtehude
10. Royal Liverpool Philharmonic Orchestra
11. John Williams
12. A pub
13. A. C. Benson
14. Neither. Handel was declared the victor on the organ and Scarlatti the victor on the harpsichord.
15. Germany
16. Howard Blake
17. *Orpheus in the Underworld*
18. Westminster Abbey
19. *The Young Person's Guide to the Orchestra*
20. A musical party thrown by Franz Schubert

🎵 Round 22: Enigmas

Score / 10

1. Hummel
2. Corelli
3. Rodrigo
4. Pärt
5. Boyce
6. Puccini
7. Wagner
8. Britten
9. Bernstein
10. Salieri

🎵 Round 23: Cinematic Sounds

Score /20

1. Malcolm Arnold
2. Camille Saint-Saëns
3. *Adagio for Strings*
4. *The Sugarland Express*
5. *A Song of Summer*
6. Robert Powell
7. *Fantasia*
8. Peter Shaffer
9. *Brassed Off*
10. *L'assassinat du Duc de Guise*
11. *Zadok the Priest*

12. Stanley Kubrick
13. Austrian
14. CBS Symphony Orchestra
15. *Der Rosenkavalier*
16. Craig Armstrong
17. Royal College of Music in London
18. *Hilary and Jackie*
19. Bernard Herrmann
20. It wasn't written for any particular film or scene.

🎵 **Round 24:** Quick Fire (Intermediate)

Score /20

1. Polyphony
2. Peter Maxwell Davies
3. Mary I and Elizabeth I
4. Canterbury Cathedral
5. Thomas Tallis
6. Lincoln Cathedral
7. Printing music and music paper
8. *Euridice*
9. King Louis XIV
10. The Chapel Royal
11. Carthage
12. *Zadok the Priest*
13. Max Bruch's *Violin Concerto No. 1*
14. Asthma
15. Violin

16. They were cousins.
17. The Duke of Saxe-Weissenfels
18. The Elector of Hanover
19. King George II
20. Dublin

 Round 25: True or False?

Score /20

1. False – they each wrote nine.
2. True
3. True
4. True – in his *Symphony No. 5*
5. False – he did write one about coffee, though.
6. True
7. True
8. True
9. False – she worked in a cigarette factory.
10. True
11. True
12. False – his parents were originally Lithuanian.
13. False – it was a protest against a nuclear reprocessing plant.
14. False – he was in Eastbourne.
15. True
16. True
17. False – he was an ambulance driver.

18. False – he was off the coast at Gravesend.
19. False – Darwin was his great-uncle.
20. True

🎵 **Round 26:** Quick Fire (Intermediate)

Score /20

1. *Orpheus and Euridice*
2. Esterhazy
3. Johann Christian Bach
4. 154
5. Cello
6. Nannerl
7. 4 years
8. Allegri's *Miserere*
9. Constanze Weber
10. 35
11. Arthur Sullivan
12. Franz Joseph Haydn
13. Ludwig van Beethoven
14. The chin rest for the violin
15. Because it was widely believed at the time that he had made a pact with the devil.
16. Typhus
17. He started to train to be a doctor.
18. Four — one on each corner of the stage
19. Fron Male Voice Choir
20. Nicola Benedetti

Round 27: The Year in Question

Score /20

1. 1858
2. 1859
3. 1862
4. 1869
5. 1865
6. 1870
7. 1876
8. 1877
9. 1878
10. 1878
11. 1881
12. 1882
13. 1883
14. 1891
15. 1894
16. 1896
17. 1898
18. 1899
19. 1900
20. 1901

𝄢 **Round 28:** In Good Voice

Score /20

1. Tenor
2. Tenor

3. Mezzo-soprano
4. Tenor
5. Countertenor
6. Soprano
7. Tenor
8. Tenor
9. Soprano
10. Soprano
11. Soprano
12. Mezzo-soprano
13. Soprano
14. Soprano
15. Soprano
16. Mezzo-soprano
17. Tenor
18. Countertenor
19. Bass-baritone
20. Bass

Round 29: Quick Fire (Intermediate)

Score /20

1. Johann Sebastian Bach, Ludwig van Beethoven, Johannes Brahms
2. Four
3. Georges Bizet's *The Pearl Fishers*
4. Nikolai Rimsky-Korsakov
5. Law

6. He was poisoned by drinking water infected by cholera.
7. *My Homeland*
8. Trains and ships
9. William Schwenck
10. *The Tales of Hoffmann*
11. Hector Berlioz and Georges Bizet
12. A music shop
13. *Turandot*
14. *Symphony No. 8*
15. Igor Stravinsky
16. Vocalise
17. The Royal College of Music
18. Gloucestershire
19. An orange plantation
20. Béla Bartók and Zoltán Kodály

🎵 **Round 30:** Mix & Match

Score /20

1. Ralph Vaughan Williams
2. Edward Elgar
3. Karl Jenkins
4. Jean Sibelius
5. Pyotr Ilyich Tchaikovsky
6. Bedřich Smetana
7. Georges Bizet
8. Sergei Rachmaninov

9. George Gershwin
10. Pietro Mascagni
11. Antonio Vivaldi
12. George Butterworth
13. Johann Sebastian Bach
14. Modest Mussorgsky
15. Ludwig van Beethoven
16. Peter Maxwell Davies
17. George Frideric Handel
18. Igor Stravinsky
19. William Walton
20. Aaron Copland

🎵 **Round 31:** Quick Fire (Intermediate)

Score /20

1. Sergei Diaghilev
2. Oranges — in his opera *The Love for Three Oranges*
3. A saw mill
4. Ischia
5. *Symphony No. 5*
6. A prepared piano
7. Coventry Cathedral
8. Muzio Clementi
9. New York Philharmonic Orchestra
10. The Manchester School
11. Dawn Upshaw
12. Russian Orthodox Church

13. Steven Isserlis
14. Minimalism
15. Benjamin Britten
16. Les Six
17. Christ Church Cathedral, Oxford
18. St Petersburg Conservatory
19. Fellow of the Royal Welsh College of Music and Drama
20. Vasily Petrenko

Round 32: True or False?

Score /20

1. False — she was only considered for canonization.
2. True
3. True
4. True
5. True
6. False — he was prolific, but not that prolific, composing 3,700 works during his lifetime.
7. True
8. True
9. True
10. False — he had written two operas by the age of 12.
11. False — he emigrated to Scandinavia.
12. True

13. False — he didn't graduate from a correspondence course in composition until he was 37.

14. False — they were separate songs written over a two-year period which were brought together and published after his death.

15. False — Jean Sibelius was Finnish.

16. True

17. True

18. False — we made up the bit about the lawnmower and the knitting needles. The other three "instruments" are true, though.

19. False — there are no gerbils in the work.

20. False — she was born in the Welsh town of Neath.

🏳 **Round 33:** Enigmas

Score /10

1. Mozart
2. Telemann
3. Smetana
4. Walton
5. Scarlatti
6. Byrd
7. Mahler
8. Borodin
9. Tallis
10. Spohr

🎵 **Round 34:** On the Box

Score /20

1. Cadbury Fruit & Nut
2. Old Spice
3. De Beers diamonds
4. British Airways
5. Hamlet cigars
6. Hovis bread
7. Levi jeans
8. Orange
9. Lloyds TSB
10. John Lewis
11. *What the Papers Say*
12. *Eurovision Song Contest*
13. *Alfred Hitchcock Presents…*
14. *The Onedin Line*
15. *Horse of the Year Show*
16. *The South Bank Show*
17. *The Lone Ranger*
18. *Monty Python's Flying Circus*
19. *The Sky at Night*
20. *The* (American) *Civil War*

Round 35: Order! Order!

Score /20

Musical Instrument Formations

1. Solo
2. Duet
3. Trio
4. Quartet
5. Quintet
6. Sextet
7. Septet
8. Octet
9. Nonet
10. Decimet

Stringed Instruments

1. Violin
2. Viola
3. Cello
4. Double bass

Operas

1. Claudio Monteverdi: *La favola d'Orfeo* (1607)
2. Christoph Willibald Gluck: *Orpheus and Eurydice* (1762)
3. Jacques Offenbach: *Orpheus in the Underworld* (1858)
4. Georges Bizet: *Carmen* (1875)
5. Giuseppe Verdi: *Otello* (1887)
6. Giacomo Puccini: *Madame Butterfly* (1904)

Round 36: Quick Fire (Fiendish)

Score /20

1. Bassoon
2. Richard Wagner
3. Oboe
4. The Hilliard Ensemble
5. Remo Giazotto
6. Franz Schubert
7. Harriet Smithson
8. University of Breslau
9. Vienna
10. Amandine-Aurore-Lucile Dupin
11. Nobody's really sure. He took it with him to the grave — but we hope that you had fun guessing
12. Mily Balakirev, Alexander Borodin, César Cui, Modest Mussorgsky and Nikolai Rimsky-Korsakov
13. Thirteen
14. Butterflies
15. Vienna Philharmonic Orchestra
16. Camille Saint-Saëns and Max Bruch
17. EMI Classics
18. A type of unaccompanied church singing where two parts of a choir sing alternately, with the second section answering the first
19. Guido d'Arezzo
20. Bermersheim, near Alzey in Germany

🎵 **Round 37:** They Come from Where?

Score /20

1. England
2. Estonia
3. Poland
4. Austria
5. Germany
6. France
7. Hungary
8. Norway
9. Spain
10. England
11. Finland
12. Russia
13. USA
14. Wales
15. Canada
16. Armenia
17. Scotland
18. Scotland
19. Belgium
20. Italy

🎵 **Round 38:** Name That Composer

Score /20

1. Edvard Grieg
2. Arthur Sullivan

3. Léo Delibes
4. Johann Strauss Jr
5. Giuseppe Verdi
6. Richard Wagner
7. Johannes Brahms
8. Max Bruch
9. Camille Saint-Saëns
10. Gabriel Fauré
11. Edward Elgar
12. Giacomo Puccini
13. Richard Strauss
14. Jean Sibelius
15. Sergei Rachmaninov
16. Claude Debussy
17. Maurice Ravel
18. Ralph Vaughan Williams
19. Frederick Delius
20. Sergei Prokofiev

🎵 Round 39: Quick Fire (Fiendish)

Score /20

1. "New Art"
2. Rheims
3. Cambrai Cathedral
4. Waltham Abbey
5. *Cantiones sacrae*
6. 55 days

7. Apollo
8. Canterbury Cathedral
9. Jean-Baptiste Lully
10. Count Giacomo Durazzo
11. Anna Girò
12. Johann Christoph Bach
13. Duke of Saxe-Weimar
14. Anna Magdalena Wilcken
15. John Taylor
16. *Rinaldo*
17. Alessandro
18. South America
19. King Frederick the Great
20. *Essay on the True Art of Playing Keyboard Instruments*

Round 40: The Year in Question

Score /20

1. 1902
2. 1904
3. 1905
4. 1908
5. 1910
6. 1911
7. 1912
8. 1913
9. 1914
10. 1917

11. 1918
12. 1919
13. 1920
14. 1922
15. 1924
16. 1926
17. 1927
18. 1933
19. 1934
20. 1935

🎼 **Round 41:** Fully Entitled

Score /20
1. Princess
2. Tsar
3. King
4. Count
5. Colonel
6. Knight
7. Emperor
8. Duke
9. Count
10. Baron
11. King
12. Prince
13. Tsar
14. Emperor
15. Duke

16. Count
17. Emperor
18. King
19. Prince
20. King

🎵 **Round 42:** Mind the Gap

Score /20

1. *Trout*
2. *Cuckoo*
3. *Bird*
4. *Goose*
5. *Lark*
6. *Magpie*
7. *Swan*
8. *Swan*
9. *Swan*
10. *Vixen*
11. *Bee*
12. *Bumblebee*
13. *Butterfly*
14. *Wasps*
15. *Duckling*
16. *Sheep*
17. *Flea*
18. *Wolf*
19. *Animals*
20. *Elephant*

🎧 **Round 43:** Odd One Out

Score /20

1. Evgeny Kissin is a pianist and all the others are cellists.
2. The cornet is a brass instrument. All the others are percussion instruments.
3. Natalie Clein is a cellist and all the others are violinists.
4. Johann Sebastian is the father. The other four are his sons.
5. *Carmen* is an opera and all of the others are ballets.
6. *Carmen* was written by Bizet; all of the other operas were composed by Puccini.
7. All of these are genuine pieces written by Erik Satie, except for *Étude on Consideration of a Striped Ocelot*, which we made up.
8. *Parsifal* because, although it's an opera by Richard Wagner, it's not part of the *Ring Cycle*.
9. All the soundtracks to these films were written by John Williams, except for *Rain Man*, which was composed by Hans Zimmer.
10. Scarlatti, Bach and Handel were all born in 1685, but Zipoli was born in 1688.
11. All these operas were composed by Wolfgang Amadeus Mozart, except for *Turandot*, which was composed by Giacomo Puccini.

12. *Otello* was written by Giuseppe Verdi, but the other three are operas written by Gioachino Rossini.

13. Camille Saint-Saëns died at the age of 86; all the other three composers died while still in their thirties.

14. Gustav Mahler was the only one of these four composers not to die in an asylum.

15. Pyotr Ilyich Tchaikovsky — all the others were members of the group of Russian composers known as "The Mighty Handful".

16. The Italian Domenico Zipoli – all of the others were Czech.

17. Heitor Villa-Lobos, because, although all five of these composers are considered to be in the Spanish "nationalist school", Villa-Lobos was actually Brazilian.

18. *The Thieving Magpie* was written by Gioachino Rossini. All of the others were by W. S. Gilbert and Arthur Sullivan.

19. The American George Gershwin – all of the others were British.

20. The German Max Bruch – all of the others were French.

🎵 **Round 44:** Quick Fire (Fiendish)

Score /20

1. Aloysia Weber
2. Pushkin
3. 14
4. 56
5. *Violin School*
6. An opera company
7. 37
8. 144
9. Niccolò Paganini
10. He was a doctor.
11. 1833
12. Jean Françaix
13. Quarter-notes
14. 2,065
15. 37
16. 17
17. *A Life for the Tsar*
18. Nikolai Rimsky-Korsakov
19. Nadezhda von Meck
20. Five

🔲 **Round 45:** Enigmas

Score /10

1. Tartini
2. Liszt

3. Grieg
4. Reger
5. Delibes
6. Bizet
7. Strauss
8. Fauré
9. Monteverdi
10. Glinka

🎵 **Round 46:** Mix & Match

Score /20

1. Baroque
2. Modern
3. Romantic
4. Modern
5. Romantic
6. Modern
7. Romantic
8. Classical
9. Early
10. Early
11. Romantic
12. Baroque
13. Romantic
14. Modern
15. Romantic
16. Romantic
17. Early

18. Modern
19. Baroque
20. Romantic

🎹 Round 47: Order! Order!

Score /20

1. Hildegard of Bingen (1098)
2. Claudio Monteverdi (1567)
3. Henry Purcell (1659)
4. Johann Sebastian Bach (1685)
5. Franz Josef Haydn (1732)
6. Wolfgang Amadeus Mozart (1756)
7. Ludwig van Beethoven (1770)
8. Johann Strauss Sr (1804)
9. Felix Mendelssohn (1809)
10. César Franck (1822)
11. Max Bruch (1838)
12. Jules Massenet (1842)
13. Edvard Grieg (1843)
14. Edward Elgar (1857)
15. Igor Stravinsky (1882)
16. George Gershwin (1898)
17. Dmitri Shostakovich (1906)
18. Samuel Barber (1910)
19. Philip Glass (1937)
20. Patrick Hawes (1958)

🎵 Round 48: Quick Fire (Fiendish)

Score /20

1. Director of the National Conservatory of Music
2. 21 years: Johann Strauss Sr was born in 1804 and Johann Strauss Jr was born in 1825
3. A retirement home for musicians, which he had built in Milan
4. Five years: Johannes Brahms was born in 1833 and Max Bruch was born in 1838
5. Gabriel Fauré
6. A solicitor's office
7. Edward Elgar's publisher, Augustus Jaeger
8. The Cat
9. Vienna State Opera
10. *Aleko*
11. The highest mark in the institution's history: A++++
12. Dr Nikolai Dahl
13. Trombone
14. Thomas F. Ward
15. Eric Fenby
16. Arnold Schoenberg
17. Boston Symphony Orchestra
18. Kaplan
19. *Lady Macbeth of the Mtsensk District*
20. Lowestoft

🎵 **Round 49:** Mix & Match

Score /20

1. Antonio Salieri
2. Arnold Schoenberg
3. Bedřich Smetana
4. Franz Liszt
5. Frederick Delius
6. Gregorio Allegri
7. Hector Berlioz
8. Henryk Górecki
9. Isaac Albéniz
10. Jacopo Peri
11. Jacques Offenbach
12. Johannes Brahms
13. Louis Spohr
14. Maurice Ravel
15. Mikhail Glinka
16. Modest Mussorgsky
17. Nikolai Rimsky-Korsakov
18. Orlando Gibbons
19. Paul McCartney
20. Ralph Vaughan Williams

🎵 **Round 50:** On the Street Where You Live

Score /20

1. George Frideric Handel
2. Ralph Vaughn Williams
3. Edvard Greig
4. Sir David Willcocks
5. Antonín Dvořák
6. Peter Warlock
7. Johann Strauss Sr
8. Frederick Delius
9. Frédéric Chopin
10. Sir Malcolm Sargent
11. Sergei Rachmaninov
12. Edward Elgar
13. Giacomo Puccini
14. Thomas Beecham
15. Niccolò Paganini
16. Eric Fenby
17. Felix Mendelssohn
18. Sir Adrian Boult
19. Claude Debussy
20. Charles Avison

🎼 **Round 51: Whose Aria Is It Anyway?**

Score /20

1. Giacomo Puccini: *La Bohème*
2. Giuseppe Verdi: *La traviata*
3. Giuseppe Verdi: *Il trovatore*
4. Pyotr Ilyich Tchaikovsky: *Eugene Onegin*
5. Giuseppe Verdi: *Nabucco*
6. George Frideric Handel: *Semele*
7. Camille Saint-Saëns: *Samson and Delilah*
8. Giuseppe Verdi: *Rigoletto*
9. George Gershwin: *Porgy and Bess*
10. Giacomo Puccini: *Tosca*
11. Wolfgang Amadeus Mozart: *Don Giovanni*
12. Gaetano Donizetti: *L'elisir d'amore*
13. Christoph Willibald Gluck: *Orpheus and Euridice*
14. Wolfgang Amadeus Mozart: *The Magic Flute*
15. Giacomo Puccini: *La rondine*
16. Giuseppe Verdi: *Rigoletto*
17. Wolfgang Amadeus Mozart: *The Marriage of Figaro*
18. Wolfgang Amadeus Mozart: *Don Giovanni*
19. Georges Bizet: *Carmen*
20. Giacomo Puccini: *Madame Butterfly*

🔊 **Round 52: Cinematic Sounds**

Score /20

1. *The Silence of the Lambs*
2. *Platoon*

3. *A Clockwork Orange*
4. *Trainspotting*
5. *The Ladykillers*
6. *Bridget Jones's Diary*
7. *Out of Africa*
8. *The Shawshank Redemption*
9. *A Beautiful Mind*
10. *Natural Born Killers*
11. *A Room with a View*
12. *Bend It Like Beckham*
13. *Shine*
14. *Brassed Off*
15. *Babe*
16. *2001: A Space Odyssey*
17. *Billy Elliot*
18. *Pretty Woman*
19. *What's Opera, Doc?*
20. *Apocalypse Now*

🎼 Round 53: Operatic Dons

Score /20

1. *Lucrezia Borgia*
2. *Così fan tutte*
3. *The Gondoliers*
4. *The Barber of Seville*
5. *Les Indes galantes*
6. *La forza del destino*

7. *The Marriage of Figaro*
8. *The Barber of Seville*
9. *Les Indes galantes*
10. *La finta semplice*
11. *The Marriage of Figaro*
12. *Fidelio*
13. *Don Giovanni*
14. *Carmen*
15. *Koanga*
16. *Don Giovanni*
17. *Fidelio*
18. *La finta semplice*
19. *Don Quixote*
20. *Don Carlo, La forza del destino, Emani*

🎵 Round 54: Mix & Match

Score /16
Christmas carols:
1. Felix Mendelssohn
2. Gustav Holst
3. Benjamin Britten
4. Ralph Vaughan Williams
5. Victor Hely-Hutchinson

Classical music eras:
1. Early
2. Baroque
3. Classical

4. Romantic
5. Modern

The Planets Suite:
1. War
2. Peace
3. Jollity
4. Magic
5. Old Age
6. Mysticism

Round 55: The Year in Question

Score /20
1. 1936
2. 1938
3. 1942
4. 1947
5. 1948
6. 1953
7. 1958
8. 1962
9. 1971
10. 1972
11. 1975
12. 1976
13. 1985
14. 1987

15. 1989
16. 1990
17. 1992
18. 1995
19. 1996
20. 1999

🎵 **Round 56:** Enigmas

Score /10
1. *Moonlight Sonata*
2. *The Four Seasons*
3. *The Rite of Spring*
4. *Eine kleine Nachtmusik*
5. *Carmen*
6. *The Ring Cycle*
7. *Carmina Burana*
8. *1812 Overture*
9. *Blue Danube*
10. *Peer Gynt*

🏛 **Round 57:** Order! Order!

Score /20
Musical notes:
1. Breve
2. Semibreve
3. Minim

4. Crotchet
5. Quaver
6. Semiquaver
7. Demisemiquaver
8. Hemidemisemiquaver

The *Ring Cycle*:
1. Das Rheingold
2. Die Walküre
3. Siegfried
4. Götterdämmerung

Stravinsky:
1. Russia
2. Switzerland
3. France
4. USA

Ballets:
1. *Giselle*
2. *Coppélia*
3. *The Sleeping Beauty*
4. *Pulcinella*

🎵 Round 58: Name that Composer

Score /20
1. Francis Poulenc
2. George Gershwin

3. Aaron Copland
4. William Walton
5. Dmitri Shostakovich
6. Benjamin Britten
7. Leonard Bernstein
8. Arvo Pärt
9. John Tavener
10. Philip Glass
11. John Rutter
12. Karl Jenkins
13. Paul McCartney
14. Ludovico Einaudi
15. Joby Talbot
16. John Williams
17. John Barry
18. Howard Shore
19. James Horner
20. Hans Zimmer

Round 59: Heavenly Music

Score /24

1. Sagittarius
2. Sagittarius
3. Taurus
4. Capricorn
5. Scorpio
6. Leo

7. Aquarius
8. Pisces
9. Gemini
10. Libra
11. Leo
12. Cancer
13. Gemini
14. Pisces
15. Aries
16. Virgo
17. Cancer
18. Aquarius
19. Virgo
20. Capricorn
21. Scorpio
22. Aries
23. Libra
24. Taurus

☯ Round 60: Anything Goes

Score /20

1. Northern Sinfonia
2. RCA Victor – all of the other three are part of Universal Music Group.
3. Klaus Heymann
4. John Brunning – as lead guitarist in the 1970s band Mungo Jerry.

5. Paul Mealor
6. Gareth Malone
7. John Williams
8. André Rieu
9. China
10. Robin Gibb
11. The law
12. Katherine Jenkins
13. Tchaikovsky's *Nutcracker*
14. True
15. *Les Misérables*
16. Felix Mendelssohn
17. Johannes Brahms
18. William Walton
19. Three
20. *The Last Rose of Summer*

WHERE TO FIND OUT MORE ABOUT CLASSICAL MUSIC

If this book has whetted your appetite to find out more, one of the best ways to discover what you like about classical music is to tune in to Classic FM. We broadcast 24 hours a day across the UK on 100-102 FM, on Digital Radio, online at www.classicfm.com, on Sky Channel 0106, on Virgin Media channel 922 and on FreeSat channel 721. We play a huge breadth of different classical music each week. You can also download an App from the iTunes App Store, which will enable you to listen to Classic FM on the move on your iPhone, iPod or iPad.

As well as being able to listen online, you will find a host of interactive features about classical music, composers and musicians on our website, classicfm.com. When we first turned on Classic FM's transmitters 20 years ago, we changed the face of classical music radio in the UK for ever. Two decades later, we are doing the same online.

If books are more your thing than websites, then we would very much like to recommend three companion volumes to *The Classic FM Quiz Book*, all of which are published by Elliott & Thompson. The first, *Classic Ephemera*, is a musical miscellany, packed with all manner of handy information: telling trivia, curious quotes and fascinating facts. The second, *The Classic FM Hall of Fame*, profiles the 300 greatest classical works and their composers – as voted by Classic FM listeners. And the third, *Everything You Ever Wanted To Know About Classical Music … But Were Too Afraid To Ask* takes readers on a journey through the history of classical music, while also demystifying the genre's terminology and traditions.

If you would like to delve far, far deeper into the subject, the universally acknowledged authority on the subject is *The New Grove Dictionary of Music and Musicians*. The original version was edited by Sir George Grove in the late 1800s, with the eminent musicologist Stanley Sadie editing the later editions (between 1980 and 1995). But be warned – this is a weighty tome, running to 20 hardback volumes with around 29,000 separate articles.

In truth, this massive resource is far more detailed than most music lovers would ever need; a more manageable reference book is *The Concise Oxford Dictionary of Music*, edited by Michael Kennedy (published by Oxford Reference), or *The Penguin Companion to Classical Music*, edited by Paul Griffiths (published by Penguin). Paul Griffiths has also written *A Concise History of Western Music* (published by Cambridge University Press) – a highly readable discussion of the way in which classical music has evolved over time.

The DK Eyewitness Companion to Classical Music, edited by John Burrows (published by Dorling Kindersley), is a very colourful and reliable source of information on the chronology of classical music. Howard Goodall delves into five episodes that changed musical history, including the invention of musical notation and the creation of the recording industry, in his excellent book *Big Bangs* (published by Vintage). For a slightly quirkier walk through the subject, we recommend *Stephen Fry's Incomplete & Utter History of Classical Music*, which is published by Macmillan and is based on the award-winning Classic FM radio series of the same name, written by Tim Lihoreau.

Other excellent general guides to classical music include: *The Rough Guide to Classical Music*, edited by Joe Staines (published by Rough Guides); *The Encyclopedia of Music* by Max Wade-Matthews and Wendy Thompson (published by Hermes House); *Good Music Guide* by Neville Garden (published by Columbia Marketing); *The Chronicle of Classical Music* by Alan Kendall (published by Thames & Hudson); *The Lives & Times of The Great Composers* by Michael Steen (published by Icon); *The Lives of the Great Composers* by Harold C. Schonberg (published by Abacus); and *Music for the People: The Pleasures and Pitfalls of Classical Music* by Gareth Malone (published by Collins), whose television series on singing are fast making him a national treasure. If you ever happen across a copy of either of Jeremy Nicholas's two splendid books, *The Classic FM Guide to Classical Music* (published by Pavilion) and *The Classic FM Good Music Guide* (published by Hodder & Stoughton), then you should snap them up. Both are sadly out of print at the moment.

Three brilliant books on the subject of opera are *The DK Eyewitness Guide to Opera* (published by Dorling Kindersley); *The Good Opera Guide* by Denis Forman (published by Phoenix); and *The Rough Guide to Opera* by Matthew Boyden (published by Rough Guides).

For younger classical music lovers or discoverers, *The Story of Classical Music* and *Famous Composers* are both published by Naxos Audiobooks. These titles are aimed at 8- to 14-year-olds and contain musical excerpts and CD-ROM elements.

The very best way to find out more about which pieces of classical music you like is by going out and hearing a live performance for yourself. There is simply no substitute for seeing the whites of the eyes of a talented soloist as he or she performs a masterpiece on a stage only a few feet in front of you. If you are a first-time attender, then before you leave home, make sure that you read our guide to going to a live classical concert in our book *Everything You Ever Wanted To Know About Classical Music ... But Were Too Afraid To Ask*.

Classic FM has a series of partnerships with orchestras across the country: the Royal Scottish National Orchestra, Northern Sinfonia, the Royal Liverpool Philharmonic Orchestra, the Orchestra of Opera North, the Philharmonia Orchestra and the London Symphony Orchestra. To see if they have a concert coming up near you, log onto our website at classicfm.com and click on the "Concerts and Events" section. It will also include many of the other classical concerts – both professional and amateur – that are taking place near to where you live.

Happy listening!

ACKNOWLEDGEMENTS

Enormous thanks are due to Global Radio's Founder and Executive President, Ashley Tabor; to Group Chief Executive, Stephen Miron; to Director of Broadcasting, Richard Park; and to Chairman Sir Charles Allen CBE, each of whom has given us unstinting encouragement and support.

Among the Classic FM programming team, we must thank Nick Bailey, Jamie Beesley, Fiona Bowden, John Brunning, Stuart Campbell, Chris Chilvers, Lucy Chisholm-Batten, Lucy Coward, Jamie Crick, Chloe Faulkner, Nick Ferrari, Howard Goodall, Matt Gubbins, Owen Hopkin, Sam Jackson, Bob Jones, Jane Jones, Myleene Klass, Laurence Llewelyn-Bowen, Kyle Macdonald, David Mellor, Anne-Marie Minhall, Jenny Nelson, Phil Noyce, Bill Overton, Nicholas Owen, Emma Oxborrow, Clare Patterson, Alexandra Philpotts, Dan Ross, Mel Spencer, Lloyd Stas, John Suchet, Margherita Taylor, Alan Titchmarsh and Andrew Wright. Thanks also to Matt Rennie, Giles Pearman, Andrea Flamini, Felix Meston, Andy Chilcott and Caeshia St Paul.

Once again, we are incredibly grateful to Lorne Forsyth, Olivia Bays and Alex Spears at our publishers Elliott & Thompson for guiding us through the process of getting this book into print with enormous enthusiasm and good humour.

ABOUT THE AUTHORS

Darren Henley is the Managing Director of Global Radio's national classical music station, Classic FM. The author of twenty-three books about classical music and musicians, he is the recipient of Sony Radio Academy Awards, Arqiva Commercial Radio Awards, New York Festival Awards and a Grammy Award nomination. In 2012, he was awarded the Making Music/Sir Charles Groves Prize for his outstanding contribution to British Music. He has advised ministers in successive governments about music and cultural education, writing two major independent reviews for the Department for Education and the Department for Culture, Media and Sport. He is a Fellow of the Royal Society of Arts, of the London College of Music and of the Radio Academy; an Honorary Fellow of Canterbury Christ Church University and of Trinity Laban Conservatoire of Music and Dance; an Honorary Member of the Royal Northern College of Music; and a Companion of the Chartered Management Institute. He studied Politics at the University of Hull.

Tim Lihoreau is the presenter of the UK's most listened-to classical music breakfast programme, *Classic FM's More Music Breakfast*, which can be heard across the UK every weekday morning between 6am and 9am. He previously hosted Classic FM's weekend breakfast programme. As the station's Creative Director, Tim has won a multitude of awards for his radio writing and production on both sides of the Atlantic, as well as being the author of fourteen books.

Aside from writing about classical music, Tim has penned two humorous books called *Modern Phobias* (translated into eleven languages) and *Schadenfreude*, which both take a wry look at some of the peccadilloes of 21st-century life. With a degree in music from the University of Leeds, Tim worked as a professional pianist and at a classical and jazz record label before moving into radio. Along with his wife, he runs three amateur choirs in his home village in Cambridgeshire and regularly plays the organ at his local church.

ALSO PUBLISHED BY CLASSIC FM AND ELLIOTT & THOMPSON:

Beethoven: The Man Revealed
by John Suchet

Classic Ephemera: A Classical Music Miscellany
by Darren Henley and Tim Lihoreau

The Classic FM Hall of Fame
by Darren Henley, Tim Lihoreau and Sam Jackson

Everything You Ever Wanted To Know About Classical Music …
But Were Too Afraid To Ask
by Darren Henley and Sam Jackson

Schadenfreude: The Little Book of Black Delights
by Tim Lihoreau